Interpretations of British Politics

By the same author

Nationalisation in British Industry (Jonathan Cape, 1966 and 1973)

The Politics of the Firm (Martin Robertson, 1978)

The Nation-State (edited) (Martin Robertson, 1981)

Party Ideology in Britain (edited with A. W. Wright) (Routledge, 1988)

Interpretations of British Politics

The image and the system

Leonard Tivey

Head of Department of
Political Science and International Studies
University of Birmingham

HARVESTER · WHEATSHEAF

NEW YORK   LONDON   TORONTO   SYDNEY   TOKYO

First published 1988 by
Harvester · Wheatsheaf
66 Wood Lane End, Hemel Hempstead
Hertfordshire HP2 4RG
A division of
Simon & Schuster International Group

Printed and bound in Great Britain by
Billing & Sons Ltd, Worcester

British Library Cataloguing in Publication Data

Tivey, Leonard, *1926–*
Interpretations of British politics : the
image and the system.
1. Great Britain. Politics, 1860–1987
I. Title
320.941
ISBN 0-7450-0171-8
ISBN 0-7450-0547-0 Pbk

1 2 3 4 5 92 91 90 89 88

to
Melbourne, Derbyshire

Contents

Preface

The purpose of this book is twofold. Its primary task is to explain the main general interpretations of British politics put forward between 1860 and the present time. Its secondary role is to comment on these interpretations and to diagnose an emerging interpretation. It is therefore a contribution to the 'general theory' of British politics, not a study of its actual operations. The method and assumptions used are discussed in the introduction (Chapter 1) and need not be expounded here.

The existence of the material on which the book is based shows that there is already a disposition to generalise about the British political system. Students, teachers, and other readers are much concerned with wide assertions, with gross simplifications. This book is intended to serve as an introduction at this level, and in doing so to make clear, first, that there exists a variety of such general accounts; and secondly, that there is an evolution in these matters. It hardly need be said that readers should go on from this introduction to study the primary authorities themselves. Moreover, this discussion of generalising about British politics is not intended to replace other approaches. Knowledge and understanding of history, of institutions, of actual behaviour and of wider political theory are all necessary, and may be acquired from many excellent texts and special studies already available.

A word of apology is necessary. The central chapters of this book deal with recent and contemporary interpretations. Many of the authors whose views are there discussed are still vigorously active. The enterprise may thus contribute to 'the gentle art of making enemies'. The apology is therefore to anyone who feels misrepresented, neglected or wrongly classified.

The book was written in the mid-1980s. I am indebted to my students of this period, who were the (often unconscious) stimulus to much that I have written. Among my colleagues I am particularly grateful to Cornelia Navari, Melville Currell, and Anthony Wright for constructive advice. To Marjorie Tivey I owe editorial guidance. For excellent typing I am again indebted to Marjorie Davies and Frances Landreth. I have tried to write coolly and in an academic manner; however, my private preferences may show through. Readers of Chapter 6 should be warned that, though I discern an emerging interpretation there, I do not like it very much. It remains my view that rulers should be content to govern a society, rather than manage an organisation. In any case, all the biasses, misrepresentations and other errors are my own fault.

The work is dedicated to the small town in south Derbyshire where I was born and brought up.

Leonard Tivey
University of Birmingham
January 1988

1 Introduction: The Image and the System

To interpret is, by one definition, to bring out the meaning of something. In this book the 'interpretations' to be reviewed are attempts to bring out the meaning of British politics. These interpretations will be gathered from various writings which have summarised, generalised or made judgments about political events and procedures in Britain. It will include therefore discussion of the constitution and of wider political processes; of reform and adaptation; of criticism and of exposition.

The interpretations in question are those concerned with the period from 1860 to 1987. There will be no attempt to recount the history of the period in general, though there will be reference to some episodes for purposes of illustration. What are here examined are views and analyses, not the events which were their prior material. The task is to explain the explanations.

Of course, the interpretations cannot be completely divorced from the events—time and circumstances are relevant to understanding them. Moreover, the interpretive school to which the book itself conforms is that of 'operative concepts', or 'operative ideals' as Lindsay[1] called them. That is to say, the views of the authors are taken to be of some influence: what they have said has to some extent become operative. Their ideas may not have reached the masses or the media at a single bound, but they have gained currency among those who study politics, and diluted and distorted they have reached the practitioners.

Before going any further, however, some disclaimers had better be issued. The interpretations are not ideologies, properly so-called. Still less are they political theories or philosophies of broad implications. The generalisation involved in the act of interpretation is generalisation about British affairs only. Examples illustrate the distinction. The idea of the Divine Right of kings was a theory of legitimacy that could (conceivably) be applied to *any* kingdom. Similarly the philosophy of Thomas Hobbes about sovereign power was relevant to any polity. But the notion of the Parliamentary forces—that in England specifically English laws had been usurped by the King—was an interpretation: it depended on a perception (or an invention) of how things were done in England. Again, the Whig view of the eighteenth-century balanced constitution was an interpretation of how things had come to be in Britain as a result of the fortunate post-1688 settlements; it was misapplied by Montesquieu and others as a theory of universal relevance about the proper separation of powers.

On the other hand, hard information about institutions, even crucial ones like the Cabinet, or about behaviour such as that of voters, is only relevant insofar as it affects general interpretations. Moreover, it is the way such information has been received and fitted into existing conceptions that is important. No new data will be presented, nor will existing data be re-analysed. It is the interpretations themselves that constitute the subject-matter.

There arise, however, problems of presentation. The question of the vocabulary of political studies, and the mechanical metaphors common in the twentieth century, are discussed in Chapter 6. There is no way in which such familiar language can be avoided in this account. Nevertheless there will be an attempt to avoid the constraints it imposes, by widening the range of metaphor. Thus words from other arts, like 'picture' or 'vision' or 'scene' will be used to describe interpretations; or again, terms like 'theme' and 'discord' will be employed. They will be used loosely; indeed, that is their purpose—to loosen up the exposition. Perhaps this device will go a little way to avoid the danger of explaining one interpretation in terms appropriate to others.

In particular, as the sub-title of the book indicates, the term 'image' is used to denote the consequence of an interpretation. As stated, the interpreters are mainly scholars, academic and otherwise, and high-quality journalists. Their writings become known, or half-known, and so a vaguely-formed view spreads around. This is the image. It is a set of assumptions about 'the system' (or 'the constitution' in earlier usage) and how it works. The relations of these two notions are further discussed in Chapter 2.

No close comparison between one interpretation and another will be possible. They do not fit. They do not focus on the same phenomena. However, in order to provide some form of linkage, a set of three questions will be posed at intervals through the book.

(i) Does the interpretation involve some indication of a split level in the system? For want of better terms, is some form of 'high politics' and of 'low politics' stated or implied? Or are the arrangements seen rather as a unity or a continuum?

(ii) Alternatively, is there a sharp turning point in the historical development—in the past, or envisaged in the foreseeable future? A major crisis or revolution would be such a change. Or is the vision one of evolution only?

(iii) In any case, do the values implicit in the interpretation show what is better or worse? What, if anything, constitutes progress?

These three questions cannot all be answered for every interpretation, but they help to draw attention to underlying structures in the interpretations.

Two forms of exposition are employed. In Chapters 2 and 3 a sequence of writings is examined, primarily in historical order. There is an overlap in time between the two chapters, however, to take account of the arrival of new themes. In the succeeding Chapters 4 and 5 there is a different procedure. Both are concerned with interpretations of the system during the period 1945–87, and instead of a chronological series there is a classification of interpretative themes, or schools of thought.

This is probably the most perilous stage of the expedition. For one thing, all classifications are hazardous: life does not fit conveniently into boxes. So it might be possible to present the various opinions as some sort of seamless web, or maybe a miscellaneous collection of contrasting and overlapping views. Such a method would do less violence to reality, for indeed setting up a classification suggests divisions which are certainly not precise. Moreover, the authors themselves may reject the classifications. Most writers feel some impatience with the proposition that their best thoughts can be readily categorised, along no doubt with the thoughts of dozens of others. Was it for this that they pondered and delineated their careful expositions?

Yet the seamless web offers poor guidance to the reader. Some sort of outlines need to be glimpsed through the fog. To be authentic the groupings must be vague and tentative; they are best labelled schools or mere tendencies to emphasise the looseness of the connections. One particularly misleading practice, that of dividing ideas into two types only, 'liberal' and 'marxist', will be absolutely rejected. It is not only a gross oversimplification, (so are many of the interpretations to be considered) but it is also a sort of philosophic cold war which puts readers' minds into grooves rather than opens them out. But a more complex set of headings is worth the attempt; it offers some signposts on the way.

Indeed, the themes are not intended to correspond to ideologies, or any particular scheme or map of ideological division. It would be idle to pretend, of course, that ideologies do not have anything to do with it—that they do not lurk in the background. Indeed, how could it be otherwise? But there is much more to ideologies than the fragments which are brought into focus here. Still less do these themes or schools purport to have a correspondence with the party-political configuration. An analysis of party ideologies is another project; it is not attempted here.[2]

It is banal to point out that between the 1860s and the 1980s Britain underwent great changes in population, economy and social structure as well as in government and politics. It is relevant to such a study as this, however, that late in this period, there was academic development.

The period under consideration in the later chapters, 1945 to 1987, was one rich in political writings. The number of academic teachers and researchers in political subjects in Britain multiplied several times over. In 1945 politics (or political science, or government) was only really established in two English universities, London and Oxford, though there were individual chairs and lectureships in other places. By the 1970s it had become normal at nearly every university and polytechnic, and the output of serious scholarship matched this development. There was much quality writing by journalists and other non-academic authors; and some of the greatest contributions came from American observers.

The progress of political studies in general terms has been reflected in work about Britain. The pre-1945 era will be discussed in the next two chapters. In the early 1950s there was a movement to deeper study of government itself—to public administration. In the mid-1950s studies of elections, of parties and then of pressure groups extended the range of institutions under scrutiny. By this time such research was evolving on behaviourist and comparative lines. In the 1960s the Study of Parliament Group began a long series of detailed researches, and a controversy about the power of the Prime Minister prompted examination of that office and of the Cabinet. In some cases it was political events that obviously stimulated research into particular subjects—the rise of nationalism led to work on that strange structure, the United Kingdom; and spending cuts concentrated minds more closely on the process of public expenditure control. Thus some work was crisis-oriented; in other matters it was clearly reform-inspired.

This vast literature provided a plethora of material for such a commentary as this. Nevertheless, though they could not fail to provide sustenance, particular institutions and special studies were not the target. Generalities were what were under survey.

The final chapter of the book attempts to sum up and draw conclusions from the preceding five. It also contains a more speculative venture, an attempt to discern the emergence of yet another interpretation—'managerial nationalism'.

2 The Forerunners, 1860–1914

The political history of Britain is long, and that of its component countries longer still. The ascendancy of the civilisation built on the islands of the northeast Atlantic began with the creation of political unity in England in the late Middle Ages, and thereby the creation of a single people, a nation. The advantages of this social and political unification both in England and its later British version led to widespread admiration, and in Europe other similar systems were constructed, often slowly and painfully. By the nineteenth century this type of polity—that of a sovereign state ruling a culturally-united people—had become the ideal of a thriving new ideology, that of nationalism. For a time, indeed, an expanded version, imperialism, prevailed. By the twentieth century the nationalist ideology had triumphed in all parts of the world. The political development of the rest of the world soon led not only to the end of the imperial episode but to a relative decline of the British prototype, a change aggravated by economic competition.

The business of this book lies mainly with this latest period. Its concern is political, not social or economic. Moreover, it looks only at ideas about the system, not at the whole range of politics. In the main its interest lies with views from the inside, or at least with views that the British took notice of and learned to respect.

There is a tradition of such observations, and hence a problem of where to begin. Perhaps Henry de Bracton, who first attempted a systematic account of the laws of England in the middle of the thirteenth century, should be counted.

Perhaps the seventeenth-century theory often attributed to Sir Edward Coke, of English liberties stretching back to times immemorial, should be included. The great lawyer, Sir William Blackstone, published *Commentaries on the Laws of England* in 1765–9, devoted partly to a conservative admiration for the contrivances of the constitution. In 1784 a French author, J. L. de Lolme, published *The Constitution of England*, suggesting that the undoubted liberties of the English depended, in particular, on the separate rights of the monarchical executive and the division of the legislature into two houses.

The existence of these and other works establishes the validity of the tradition, but really they are antecedent to the present purpose. The object of this chapter is to begin the story, to establish the scene. To do this it will give an account of the views of those interpreters whose ideas survive—not perhaps as verities, or any longer as sound doctrine, but which nevertheless constituted the foundations which were rebuilt after 1945.

The most common historical analysis of political development in Britain puts primary emphasis on the theory of representation. The great periods (say the authorities) were the Old Tory era; the Whig period of the balanced constitution; and the Liberal age of popular democracy, of 'government by the people'. In the first period the people were represented, and governed, by an 'organic' relationship: it was the monarch's inherent natural connection with the people of his realm that enabled him to rule and to expect allegiance. In the Whig period, it was said, an historically fortunate series of developments had provided the country with a set of institutions which balanced one another, and enabled social forces also to balance one another. In the liberal view, at least in its radical versions, these balances were held to be unnecessary provided the people governed themselves, by electing the rulers.[1] This chapter will be concerned with how writers interpreted the politics of this period from the 1860s onwards. The succeeding chapters will consider the varying interpretations of what happened after that.

The most vivid pictures of how Britain was governed in the liberal era were drawn largely from the works of two authors, Walter Bagehot, a journalist, and A. V. Dicey, a lawyer. But before discussing their great contributions, consideration of the views of one earlier writer is necessary. To understand the character of nineteenth-century argument it is, as usual, necessary to confront the ideas of John Stuart Mill.

The first step in the trend towards popular government had been the Reform Act of 1832. It did not extend the franchise very much, but it cleared the worst anomalies and regularised the voting system. Most important, it showed the way: in spite of early attempts to treat it as a final settlement of the constitution, new claims for further reform spread in the middle of the century. At this time, therefore, there was a system in which Governments were dependent on Parliamentary support, and hence a system of 'Parliamentary government', but in which there was also a renewed debate about the extension of the franchise. This debate was conducted at a practical level—what should in fact be done next?—but it also raised fundamental questions about the proper form of government, and about its nature and purposes.

The radical movement of the 1830s and 1840s, Chartism, had made manhood suffrage its leading demand, and though the movement as such collapsed after 1848, the desire for change did not disappear. The widespread image of the political system at this time was that there existed a well-established aristocratic order, embodying principles of limitation and balance which gave it great merit; but which had to face challenge. Some appreciable change had in fact occurred, and new commercial and professional classes were gaining much political power. Given Parliamentary supremacy, already achieved in Britain, the question of the vote was crucial.[2]

John Stuart Mill's *Considerations on Representative Government* was published in 1861.[3] Mill was the most renowned radical philosopher of the age, author of *On Liberty* and other classic works. He had already made some observations on the franchise in *Thoughts on Parliamentary Reform* (1859).[4] In this pamphlet he stressed the urgency of correcting the worst anomalies of representation first. Beyond that, he thought that eventually all adults should have at least one vote, but educated, professional, and skilled people should have more—sometimes several—votes. *Representative Government* was a work of a different sort. It set out to be a treatise on principles. It aimed to begin at the beginning and to argue logically from there. Its first chapter was entitled 'To what extent forms of government are a matter of choice'.[5] Within limits, Mill answered; people must be able and willing to operate their essential procedures. What was the criterion of a good system of government? he then asked. His answer embodied the value on which his social philosophy turned—the improvement of mankind. A system of government should educate and develop the characters of the citizens. Not only should it avoid oppressing them: its own operations should make them better people. To use recent terminology, Mill believed in participatory democracy

> The only government which can fully satisfy all the exigencies of the social state is one in which the whole people participate; that any participation, even in the smallest public function, is useful; that the participation should be everywhere as great as the general degree of the improvement of the community will allow; and that nothing less can be ultimately desirable than the admission of all to a share in the sovereign power of the state.[6]

In practice, in large societies, this meant a form of representative government.

However, Mill had doubts and qualifications. General ignorance and incapacity unfitted people for representative government. There was a danger that a ruling class would retain privileges. Moreover, Mill asserted that there was also a danger of 'majority interests'. No class, he argued should be able to exercise a preponderant influence—there should be a balance between capitalists and workers. To safeguard the system he recommended an early version of proportional representation.

> But even in this democracy, absolute power, if they chose to exercise it, would rest with the numerical majority; and these would be composed of a single class, alike in biasses, prepossessions and general modes of thinking and a class, to say no more, not the most highly cultivated.[7]

Mill continued to stress the value of the franchise as an educative force: having the vote would encourage people to take an interest in public affairs. To begin with, universal instruction should precede universal suffrage, and there should be extra votes for educated people. Mill also advocated, unusually for his time, votes for women; and, contrary to most radicals, he opposed vote by secret ballot since he thought that it would encourage self-interested voting, instead of public-spirited voting. There should be some form of second chamber, to act as a check on the first. Nevertheless, Mill asserts what was the dominant belief of the century:

> The character of a representative government is fixed by the constitution of the popular House. Compared with this, all other questions relating to the form of government are insignificant.[8]

The ideas of Mill were too radical for most other political thinkers and politicians of the time. However, he commanded great respect. The manner and clarity of his arguments meant that it was necessary to take issue, to propose counter arguments. In a sense he provided a target, and so his propositions are an appropriate starting point for this chapter.

WALTER BAGEHOT

A very different approach was made later in the decade. A picture of political actuality, rather than a possible ideal, was the purpose of Walter Bagehot's *English Constitution*[9] published in 1867. Its author came from a Somerset family of bankers, was educated at University College, London, and became editor of *The Economist*. He was a literary critic and financial authority as well as a political writer. By the mid-1860s, the excitement over further electoral reform had increased, and proposals were avidly debated in Parliament and outside. It was in this atmosphere that Bagehot wrote.

Bagehot began by quoting Mill, in a somewhat sardonic way: 'On all great subjects . . . much remains to be said.'[10] He then proceeded to say more about the English constitution, and he proceeded in a way strikingly different from Mill. He said that '. . . an observer who looks at the living reality will wonder at the contrast to the paper description.'[11] So he rejected the method of beginning with basic principles. The first thing to do was to get a proper understanding of 'living reality'. Only then could the possibilities of reform be envisaged. Do not, he implied, start with an abstract model and try to argue from that, however cautiously.

He then asserted the error of two theories. First was the view that there was a division of power—'that the legislative, the executive, and the judicial powers are quite divided.' The second was the 'checks and balances' view, in which monarchy, aristocracy and democracy counteracted each other's faults.[12]

He rejected these theories because they did not embody a vital piece of analysis. Here Bagehot put forward his most important contribution; and in spite of his dislike of abstract generalities, it was a broad theory. In long-established constitutions, he said:

There are two parts (not indeed separable with microscopic accuracy, for the genius of great affairs abhors nicety of division); first, those which excite and preserve the reverence of the population—the *dignified* parts if I may so call them; and next, the *efficient* parts; those by which it, in fact, works and rules.[13]

On this great principle much of the later argument turned.

The dignified parts of the system were in Bagehot's view absolutely essential. They were not superfluous decorations. For he took a harsh view of the political capacities of most people:

The lower orders, the middle orders, are still, when tried by what is the standard of the educated 'ten thousand', narrow-minded, unintelligent, incurious. It is useless to pile up abstract words. Those who doubt should go out into their kitchens.[14]

The dignified elements of a constitution were necessarily adjusted to impress the lower orders. They were in England complicated, old and venerable. The efficient parts in contrast were new and simple. A constitution had been stumbled on which could, when needed, work better than any other system of government.

This secret efficiency derived from the unity, the 'nearly complete fusion' of the executive and the legislature. The link was the Cabinet: 'a hyphen which joins, a buckle which fastens, the legislative part of the state to the executive part of the state.'[15] Hence Bagehot's conception of the system was one of *cabinet government*, rather than Parliamentary government or the American system of Presidential government.

All this was found in the first chapter of *The English Constitution*. After this dramatic opening much of the rest of the book tended to anticlimax. There were two chapters on the Monarchy, which extolled its power to excite reverence, and to act as a disguise, and which contained the celebrated formulation of the right of the monarch to 'be consulted, the right to encourage, the right to warn.'[16] He noted that the House of Lords also attracted reverence, but since it knew after the events of 1832 that it could be overcome (by the creation of new peers) it conducted itself accordingly. It had become a revising House, not a bulwark against revolution—its danger lay not in abolition but in decline.

The House of Commons was part of the efficient constitution: indeed the 'whole life of English politics is the action and reaction between the Ministry and the Parliament.'[17] True, the Commons had other functions—to express the mind of the people; to teach society what it should know about politics; to inform the Government about grievances; and to pass legislation, including financial measures. But its primary function meant that the House lived in a state of perpetual potential choice;[18] and therefore, Bagehot thought, party was inherent to its working—was 'bone of its bone, and breath of its breath.'[19] Nevertheless he did not see, in the 1860s, party loyalties as 'up to the dogmatic level',[20] and moderation was brought about by contact with government. He then came to the issue which occasioned his book—the franchise.

He was strongly opposed to what he called 'ultra-democracy', that is one person one vote. A Parliament elected in that way would not be composed of moderates: rural areas would send an unmixed squirarchy, and urban working-class areas 'the members for the public houses'.[21] He also rejected a scheme put forward for 'voluntary constituencies' (designed in fact to achieve what would now be seen as a form of proportional representation). But—and this was as far as he was prepared to go—because the town artisans had developed an intellectual life of their own, they ought to have *some* representatives in Parliaments.[22]

In a later chapter he returned to his attack on the theory of checks and balances. The ultimate authority in the English constitution was a newly-elected House of Commons; and it was a great virtue of the system that it contained a sovereign power, single, possible and good.[23] He also elaborated the prerequisites of Cabinet government. More than intelligence was required: other national characteristics were needed, and that is why it is so rare. There must be a mutual confidence between electors; a calm national mind; and a type of rationality capable of understanding distant objects. But most of all, for Bagehot, it was the existence of deferential nations that made it possible. A numerical majority needed to abdicate in favour of its élite. England was a prime example of a deferential country; the masses deferred to their rulers, but above all they deferred to theatrical show. This respect was traditional, and if lost would not return—'if you once permit the ignorant class to begin to rule you may bid farewell to deference for ever.'[24]

Given these views, it is not surprising that Bagehot was shocked by the events of 1867. The Liberals under Gladstone were advocating moderate electoral reform, yet many shared Bagehot's fear of extending the franchise too far. Nevertheless the Reform Act was promoted by a Conservative government at the instigation of Benjamin Disraeli, and by incorporating radical amendments it extended the vote much further than anyone anticipated. In his introduction to the later edition of *The English Constitution* Bagehot admitted that he was 'exceedingly afraid of the ignorant multitude of the new constituencies.'[25] However, in the main he reserved his judgment. The Act was likely to have many great effects, but in 1871, when he wrote, he did not know what they were.

In spite of his Liberal adherence—he stood as a Liberal candidate in an election in Bridgwater, Somerset, in 1866—

Bagehot has rightly been recognised as a political philosopher in the conservative pantheon. His fear of the multitude was no doubt excessive. Yet it vividly illustrates the political scene of Victorian England—the image which political writers presented to themselves and to others. The great minds of the time saw the inadequacies and the passions of the masses as the problem for democracy. Some were persuaded that there were plenty of sensible working people; some put their trust in more education (and the great Education Act of 1870 followed); others thought that new devices such as special franchises might help.

Bagehot wrote in a brilliant style, full of fine and memorable phrases; and his constitutional analysis has certainly illuminated the operation of the system, then and for many years afterwards. Indeed, the influence of the book on succeeding generations, and its acceptance as an authoritative guide, made it come true where it was not correct at the time—in his account of the monarch's role for example. Yet *The English Constitution* did nothing to calm the fears of the Victorians. It reminded them forcibly that their civilisation as well as their constitution was founded on confidence, and none too secure a confidence at that.

Bagehot's other main political work, called *Physics and Politics*[26] was published in 1872. The title is misleading: 'biology and politics' might be nearer the mark, but even that is not a real description. He wanted to explain the course of evolution in societies. His sources for the work include Darwinian evolution, but he ranged much wider into social psychology and anthropology. The doctrine of 'survival of the fittest' is used to explain not merely the survival of individuals or species, but of human groups or nations. Mankind had passed through three stages: primitive or preliminary; then a customary age, in which societies were held together by strong government and the power of imitation; and then a third stage in which choice and government by discussion were possible.

Physics and Politics is a work of general theory and so not directly within the scope of this book. Perhaps its most relevant passages are those where Bagehot stresses the importance of imitation in societies,[27] for English deference can be interpreted as one of its forms. Whether it is consistent with his panic about the franchise, however, is not so clear, for he has no real explanation for the emergence of societies of the third form, and hence no theory about their possible breakdown. His spiritual home was with fundamental conservative pessimism—the instinct that society was hard to understand, difficult to maintain, and liable to break down quite easily. So reflected in Bagehot, and in the image of politics he presented, is the paradox of Victorian progress—the pride and confidence in achievement matched always by the fear that social forces were about to check or even destroy its foundations.

Critics have taken their toll of some of Bagehot's propositions. His originality has been questioned—the views about the separation of powers and the balanced constitution which he attacked were not in fact the received wisdom of the age. He expressed them in extreme forms the better to destroy straw men. The crucial importance of the Cabinet had also been noted by others. However, Bagehot characterized the Cabinet as a committee of the House of Commons, and this was surely misleading. The powers and functions of the Cabinet were derived from the monarchy, and never delegated by the Commons. True, members of the Cabinet are all in Parliament, and this provides the link; they cannot survive without the loyal support of a majority in the Commons (though this means that in practice they control Parliament). But they are not a mere committee. His prescription for the monarchy anticipated rather than described the situation. Similarly his view of the weakness of the House of Lords had to be established later, in the constitutional crisis of 1910–11. On the other hand, though he supported the party system in Parliament, he did not foresee its extension either in terms of loyalty and discipline or in countrywide organisation.

However, the real question must be with his fundamental principle, the dichotomy of dignified and efficient parts of the constitution. It flows from his social analysis, for the dignified elements were in his view mainly concerned to impress the masses; the informed elite understood the realities of the efficient mechanism and herein government by discussion was possible. Yet he surely exaggerated the credulity of the one and the rationality of the other. To a degree the élite, too, deferred to the symbolism and mysticism of constitutional forms; and the capacity to grasp plain practicalities (even if not universal) extended well beyond what was implied by his educated 'ten thousand', even in the 1860s.

It is opportune to note at this juncture why Bagehot's concepts of 'dignified' and 'efficient' elements do not match the 'image' and 'system' in the sub-title of this book. The image is created by analysts, philosophers and interpreters, sophisticates all; it includes *both* dignified and efficient parts; indeed Bagehot's dichotomy is itself such an image. The system is the subject-matter of the image; it no doubt exists in reality, but it is too extensive, too complex, too fast-changing to be observed except through the simplifying lens provided by the interpreters. And since the practitioners all need, as they operate, simplified guidance, then too the images become in turn, part of the system.

In spite of all qualifications, Bagehot set the tenor of discussion of the political system for fifty years—or indeed beyond. Even in the contemporary world his message lives. More: *The English Constitution* is the model for works which followed. It set the style for the type of general analysis with which this study is concerned.

THE DEBATE CONTINUED

This period of high controversy brought of course, many other contributions besides that of Bagehot. A much longer and solider work also first published in 1867 was *The Government of England*[28] by W. E. Hearn, of the University of Melbourne, Australia. This was a formal treatise, expounding its subject in historical and legal detail, and it seems to have provided sustenance for serious scholars for many years. The author stressed the continuity of history—the 'Constitution of England under Queen Victoria is, indeed, the very Constitution under which the Confessor ruled and which the Conqueror swore to obey.'[29] He was well aware of the importance of the presence of Ministers in Parliament, and of their role there;[30] but he did not make it the key to understanding the system. Nor did he make much of the legal sovereignty of Parliament. In spite of the respect it earned, Hearn's book never attracted the following of Bagehot's or Dicey's works, and it now deserves little more than dutiful acknowledgement.

More eloquent and more blunt was the reaction of Thomas Carlyle, whose attitude to the reform of 1867 was summed up in the title of his pamphlet, *Shooting Niagara*[31]—a foolhardy enterprise.

A much more lasting and profound contribution occasioned by the debate on democracy came from a different source. In 1869 there was published a book of social comment by Matthew Arnold, *Culture and Anarchy*.[32] Arnold was a poet, a classical scholar educated at Oxford and son of Thomas Arnold, the great headmaster of Rugby School. His interests as a literary critic led him into commentary on social and political affairs, and this book was part of the debates and the agonies of the decade. Arnold shared to the full the anxieties of the time: indeed he found himself 'wandering between two worlds, one dead, the other powerless to be born'.[33] In *Culture and Anarchy* he saw two opposed standards: anarchy, by which he meant the spirit of doing nothing, *laissez-faire*, neglect; and culture, by which he meant not merely books and learning, but the spirit of enquiry, freedom from dogmatism, and inward reflection and imagination.[34] He used this contrast to emphasise the inadequacy of social and political developments.

More sympathetic to democratic ideas than most contemporaries, he nevertheless thought that the liberal reforms of the period achieved little positive: they were concerned with mere machinery. He termed the decaying aristocracy of the time, the Barbarians; the rising commercial middle classes he called the Philistines; and the rest were the Populace, a class of great potential but prone to violence and disorder.[35] The narrowness of middle class vision was his great despair. In England, in contrast to Germany and France, the development of the State as a means of promoting real human improvement was neglected or even opposed by many liberals. Arnold wanted it to promote a popular education dedicated to high standards, to the culture of self-betterment in the sense of imagination and understanding. The danger of democracy, for him, lay in Americanisation, that is a cult of ordinariness. Arnold was not concerned with the constitution or the political framework as such. He thought himself a Liberal 'tempered by experience, reflexion and renouncement.'[36]

The interest of his book here lies in his passionate redirection of the purpose of political activity—what would people do with their new freedoms? Instead of fearing democracy, he thought that the power of the State should be used to prepare people for it.[37] The State was the nation in its collective and corporate character and most represented its right reason. Arnold was not a remote intellectual; he was an inspector of schools, and in consequence it may be argued that he learned more of the real lives of urban working people than Mill, Bagehot, Dicey or many politicians of the time. On the whole Arnold despaired of his countrymen, but the advocacy of State action, of which he was so eloquent a herald, became part of the political scene. Not only did new voters want services; the services were necessary to make them fit members of the political community.

Though the reform of 1867 passed, and was succeeded by further extensions of the vote in 1884, the argument continued. James Fitzjames Stephen in 1873 published *Liberty Equality and Fraternity*,[38] in which he criticized sharply Mill and others, and W. H. Lecky in 1899 analysed *Democracy and Liberty*[39] without enthusiasm for democracy.

The most direct critic of democratic hopes was Sir Henry Maine. In 1885 he published *Popular Government*,[40] a collection of four essays. He began by reviewing the history of popularly-created governments in Europe and elsewhere since the French Revolution, and noticed that (the United States apart) they were marked by instability, military intervention, dictatorships and insurrections. Experience showed that popular government 'is characterized by great fragility.' Since its appearance, 'all forms of government have become more insecure . . .'[41] Governments would be overthrown by violent mobs or by the military. The system would be open to contrivance by organisers, the wire-pullers. Moreover if established, any system of universal suffrage would be hostile to technical and commercial innovation. Scientific truth would be suppressed if it challenged mass opinion.[42] A dead level of commonplace opinion would become the standard of legislation and policy. American prosperity was due not to democratic government but to universal competition. 'There has hardly ever been a community in which the weak have been pushed so pitilessly to the wall . . .'[43]

Democracy, Maine insisted, was a form of government and no more.[44] It was the government of the state by the many as opposed to the few. The question therefore was practical: did this form fulfill the duties of government better than other forms? Maine thought all experience showed that it did not. In Britain the Corrupt Practices Act of 1881, and the impartial recruitment of civil servants had reduced the 'old corruption'. But corruption could also 'consist in the directer process of legislating away the property of one class and transferring it to another. It is this last which is likely to be the corruption of these latter days.'[45]

Maine foresaw many developments, such as the rise of partisanship and the flood of legislation, surely enough. He denounced them all with eloquence and passion; indeed, though he wrote much in favour of calm and balanced judgments, he was not given to making them himself.

In fact, Maine's pleas were already too late to affect events. Nevertheless some of his arguments, and those of others like him, anticipate points made by the conservative sceptics and the market liberals described in Chapter 5. It is now necessary to give consideration not to prospects of reform, but the consequences of the reform on how the political system was conceived.

A. V. DICEY

The great Victorian lawyer, Albert Venn Dicey, played a major part in constructing the framework for political activity in the late nineteenth and early twentieth centuries. His treatise *Introduction to the Study of the Law of the Constitution*,[46] published in 1885, forcefully established doctrines which though eventually disputed nevertheless command the centre of attention and respect. The political importance of this legal tome arose from two factors. First was Dicey's analytical technique: he attempted bold simplifications, grand general principles stated with power and clarity, backed up with argument and comparison. Secondly, his book became standard reading in the education of lawyers and others concerned with politics and administration. (It is readily available, in paperback, in 1988.)[47] The study of constitutional law was, up to 1914, and to some extent afterwards, the most usual formal training for those involved in politics. Bagehot's influence came from the brilliance of his exposition; and to an extent so did that of Dicey, but in his case there was the reinforcement of writing the unavoidable text.

Dicey propounded, then, a constitution of simple principles. The first of these was the sovereignty of Parliament.[48] (In this sense Parliament implies Queen, Lords, Commons). There were no limits to the legislative authority of Parliament. Constitutional laws exist, but they were in no way superior or entrenched, and could be altered or repealed by the normal process. This extended to the election or composition of Parliament itself, and to the prolongation of an existing Parliament (i.e. the delaying of an Election). Acts of Parliament prevailed against morality, international law and the Royal prerogative. No Parliament could bind its successors.

The second principle Dicey called the rule of law.[49] By this he meant three things: (i) the supremacy of regular law, to the exclusion of prerogative or wide discretion, so that men might be punished for breaches of the law but for nothing else; (ii) the subjection of all, including state officials, to the ordinary law, rather than special jurisdictions; and (iii) constitutional laws and practices, including the protection of personal liberties, arose from ordinary law, not special enactments or declarations.

Dicey's conception of constitutional law was important. He rejected the view of de Tocqueville that 'the English constitution had no real existence.' However, since there was no formal Constitution in a single document, it had to be found elsewhere. In his view the term 'constitutional law' included law proper (some of which was in the form of Acts of Parliament, and hence written) but also 'conventions'. It comprised 'all rules which directly or indirectly affect the distribution of the sovereign power in the state.'[50] Rules might be laws or conventions. However, it was also Dicey's view that the conventions—real enough because commonly recognised—

though sustained in the main by the force of public opinion, were also sanctioned by the law and the courts. If they were breached, he thought, then in a short time those who broke them would find themselves in conflict with a legal provision.[51] For example, if the convention summoning Parliament annually were broken, then certain Acts would lapse and the Government would find itself without an army and without revenue.

However, there are many things beyond even the conventional rules which may be thought relevant to the way the country is governed. Dicey's solution to this problem has been of great significance for political understanding, and indeed for political studies. The range of institutions discussed in Dicey's treatise is very limited. The Cabinet, proclaimed by Bagehot to be the key to the system, is little mentioned. Nevertheless Dicey was full of admiration for Bagehot's exposition. He notes that his account of the nature of the Cabinet was 'in accordance with actual fact.'[52] The explanation, for Dicey, was that Bagehot and others dealt with 'political understandings' not constitutional law.[53] What they wrote was the province of political theory.

So perhaps it may be suggested that Dicey, too, was the propagator of a great dichotomy. There was on the one hand a set of constitutional arrangements, crucial and largely respected; there was on the other hand a wider political system.

This distinction was central to Dicey's account of sovereignty. The sovereignty of Parliament, which he postulated, meant the power of law-making unrestricted by any legal limit. This however is sovereignty in a legal sense only.

> But the word 'sovereignty' is sometimes employed in a political rather than in a strictly legal sense. That body is 'politically' sovereign or supreme in a state the will of which is ultimately obeyed by the citizens of the state.[54]

Dicey believed that the political sovereign in Great Britain could be simply defined—the electorate

> The matter indeed may be carried a little further, and we may assert that the arrangements of the constitution are now such as to ensure that the will of the electors shall by regular and constitutional

means always in the end assert itself as the predominant influence in the country. But this is a political, not a legal fact. The electors can in the long run always enforce their will.[55]

In this passage Dicey encapsulated the 'liberal theory' of the ideal political mechanism; and he stated that it already existed in Britain. The electorate had power in its grasp. All that was necessary, therefore, to achieve democracy was to extend the right to vote to all people. There was no other barrier.

Dicey was very far from being a radical democrat himself. Yet his affirmation of the constitutional position was surely important to that programme. There was reassurance, too, for the rising labour movement, and (to Dicey's dismay) for socialists. With a democratic electorate and a Parliamentary majority, *any* laws could be passed, *any* reforms could be achieved; no propertied interest could resist. So the emergent Labour Party could confidently choose a constitutional and Parliamentary strategy.

Dicey's other famous work was a set of lectures published in 1905 under the title *Law and Public Opinion in England*.[56] By public opinion Dicey meant those opinions that were of political influence, and a changing constitution means that wider circles might become involved. Opinion, he recognised, often sprang from interest, but this did not destroy its nature: it was not mere selfishness.[57] The forms of opinion were often derived from individual thinkers, and there were many delays in the transition from opinions being shaped to laws being changed. He suggested three periods in the nineteenth century—(i) before 1830 when old Tory ideas and legislative quiescence were dominant; (ii) a period from about 1825 to 1870 when Benthamite or individualist ideas, including *laissez-faire*, were in the ascendant; and (iii) a period of collectivism from about 1865.[58]

Dicey was well aware that no precise dating was possible and there was much overlap. However, he was convinced that some way or other, in England public opinion (the opinions of articulate people) however confused and changing, was the decisive force behind governmental actions,[59] and this was a key element in his political theory.

The constitutional views of Dicey have been much criticised. In 1933 Ivor Jennings published *The Law and the Constitution*.[60] He argued that Parliament's legal supremacy did not amount to what Dicey suggested: it was based on common law and was subject to practical limitations. Conventions were based on public opinion, or politicians' opinions (as Dicey said). However, many did not depend on legal backing,[61] as Dicey argued. Most of all, Dicey's view that there was no administrative law in England, because there were no special courts, was wrong.[62]

The critics do not always have the best of it. At least Dicey's views on Parliamentary sovereignty seem to have been sound, though few now share his ideas about administrative law. His account of opinion and law has been much criticised: his biographer, Richard Cosgrove, suggests that Dicey was no historian.[63] Dicey was a man of active political concerns himself—a Liberal who became a Liberal Unionist. He thought of himself as a Benthamite, which he interpreted to mean a believer in *laissez-faire*. His great political passion, however was Unionism—that is, opposition to Home Rule for Ireland—a view he maintained to the end of his life. In both his great works, Dicey ran great risks from his method, that of attempting bold generalisations. The risks led to mistakes on many matters. But the power and the authority of Dicey arose from the fact that the generalisations were not all that wide of the mark.

The other great constitutional lawyer of the period was Sir William R. Anson, who published *Law and Custom of the Constitution*[64] in three volumes, the first in 1886. It was a work of detail; he claimed to have done the work of a surveyor, as distinct from that of Dicey the artist.[65] He too distinguished law and custom from the 'practical working' of the constitution as described by Bagehot and by Sidney Low,[66] a later writer discussed in Chapter 3. He was less assured than Dicey about the sovereignty of Parliament, and emphasised the distinct powers and origins of the executive, in the Crown. The secret of the system lay in party government; and in later editions he noted the weakening power of Parliament.

THREE THEMES

There can be no question of closely comparing the contributions of various authors considered here. They do not use the same concepts because they are not pursuing the same purposes. However, the three questions mentioned in Chapter 1 can be asked, and thereby a few similarities and differences may be highlighted.

For a first clue, the idea of 'high' and 'low' politics is used. Do the writers employ a distinction of this approximate nature? For Walter Bagehot the answer is easy—there is an obvious distinction between high politics pursued by discussion within a restricted section of the population, and generally speaking rationally conducted. Low politics was for the rest, including much of the easily-corruptible electorate, and it was a matter of deference to show, of passion and at worst of riots and violence. There was not much prospect of change in these categories. For Dicey the distinction is not as marked, but he certainly saw two levels of effectiveness in the past. He accepted (without enthusiasm) a trend towards democracy. His definition of 'public' opinion as that which influences government led to the possibility that its basis would widen; though he thought that the impact of democracy was slow and uncertain, power was not static, and influence was not confined to a narrow governing circle.

On a second question, that of political progress (or regress) Bagehot's and Dicey's views were not fundamentally different. They admired the industrial and commercial progress of the mid-nineteenth century and its vigorous if restricted political life, and they viewed with apprehensions the risks, political and economic, of a democratic future. The fears were common to nearly all Victorians, but some, such as Mill and Arnold, were prepared to see ways in which a democracy might achieve better things and fulfill the hopes placed in it. Their criteria of progress might have had much in common, but clearly the radicals saw the *spread* of well-being as a primary goal, whereas the more conservative thinkers did not.

This affects answers to a third question: is political change marked by any sudden break, past or future, or is it a matter of continuous evolution? Though few took the romantic view of

Hearn, most observers were impressed by the degree of continuity at least since the seventeenth century. The feature of Mill and Arnold was that they felt that a degree of transformation was required, not only sharper than that wanted by more cautious spirits, but one that would affect people themselves, leading to their moral and intellectual betterment.

IMPERIALISM

The picture presented by the interpreters so far leaves something out. If the subject of their studies is British (or English) politics, then the exclusion might seem logical. Nevertheless, if the vision is to show what concerned the politicians, then more must be included—the Empire. None could avoid it. It was, for the Victorians, a set of problems; an achievement and a responsibility; above all, a fact.

Imperialism as an overt creed was much younger than the empire it extolled. It was heralded by some remarks in a speech by Benjamin Disraeli at the Crystal Palace in 1872.[67] It was much in evidence as a popular theme at the Golden and Diamond Jubilees of Queen Victoria, and its crisis came in the Boer War of 1899–1902. But its glory lived on, and though it had its greatest following in the Conservative Party, its appeal stretched well beyond—to a large part of the Liberal Party, to radicals like Sir Charles Dilke, to Fabian socialists like Sidney Webb, and to men of the far left like Robert Blatchford and H. M. Hyndman.

It involved some readjustment of vision and terminology in respect of British institutions. Great Britain became Greater Britain. Parliament was regarded as the Imperial Parliament, though its authority was delegated to numerous colonial bodies by the Colonial Laws Validity Act of 1865, by various Government of India Acts, and other statutes. Appeals from courts in the empire to the Judicial Committee of the Privy Council, in London, were possible. Executive authority in dependent colonies was typically exercised by Governors, who were appointed by the Crown on the advice of Ministers in the British government.

The Expansion of England[68] published by Sir John Seeley in 1883 was a leading text for this movement. Seeley was Professor of Modern History at Cambridge. He believed that history was properly concerned with the State, 'the growth and changes of a certain corporate society.'[69] In this light, and looked at in long perspective, the most striking fact about England was its expansion—'the extension of the English name into other countries of the globe.'[70] It was possible, Seeley agreed, that colonies would break away from the mother country; but on the other hand some sort of federal union might be created. Seeley went on to explain the history and problems of the expansion, and tried to avoid bombastic and heroic attitudes. The advantages of the 'expanded State' were not economic; the point of trying to maintain it for the future was political—to achieve the potential of parity with the United States or a reformed Russia.

Much of the argument presented by Seeley was incontrovertible: the empire, or expanded State, existed, a vast creation. But to the question of its political implications there was no clear answer. Federal unity was in truth impossible. Some advocated economic unity instead, by a system of tariff preference. The only overarching political institution to emerge was the occasional Imperial Conference, a merely consultative body. Nevertheless there can be no doubt that for the nineteenth and the early part of the twentieth century, the empire and its sustenance occupied a great part of the political scenery. Not everyone was an imperialist; but no political creed or programme could ignore the problems of empire.

The necessary solution was to regard the Crown and Parliament in London as embodying inherent authority. Liberal democrats might regard the right to rule as derived from the will of the people; but the people involved were the people of the United Kingdom, not the peoples of the empire. No such ideology could fit their case. In fact parts of the empire developed their own systems of self-government, and indeed became internally democratic more rapidly than Britain itself—they lacked the indigenous aristocratic tradition. In the dependent colonies and in India, no such developments occurred at this time. For most British people no inconsistency arose. Belief in mass democracy and social reform in Britain, and imperial rule beyond, co-existed well into the twentieth century.

3 Further Anticipations 1900–39

The early years of the twentieth century in Britain can be characterised as the period of democratic arrival. Instead of an atmosphere of fear and apprehension, there emerged a concern with democracy's practical realities. 'No one . . . can doubt' wrote Dicey 'that by 1900 . . . the English constitution had been transformed into something like a democracy.'[1] Something like, perhaps: there were still many steps to be taken. There was an approximation to householder suffrage, but it was not available for women—'votes for women' was a new crusade in the twentieth century, and manhood suffrage itself was not achieved until 1918. Moreover, the first decade culminated in constitutional crisis over the Lords. But indeed new issues and new outlooks began to dominate political analysis. Writers began to concern themselves not with the hypothetical possibilities of democracy in Britain, but with its realities and with its consequences: new expectations of the political system were emerging.

One orthodox text deserves more than a passing glance in this context. *The Governance of England*[2] by Sidney Low was published in 1904. Low was a journalist, of Hungarian descent, and had held an academic post in history at Kings College, London. His book was intended to bring up to date the works of earlier writers, including Bagehot and Dicey; and it attempted to describe the actual operation of the political and constitutional system, as distinct from the formal or even (in Dicey's sense) the conventional. He seems to have accepted the leading ideas of both Bagehot and Dicey—the ceremonial activities of government attract reverence, while there is a 'more or less unnoticed' efficient element doing the work;[3] he accepts the notion of conventions; and he begins his account with the Cabinet.

He stresses the importance of Cabinet responsibility—that, historically Parliament asserted its power by ensuring that Ministers (and not the monarch or other appointees of his) accepted responsibility for government. The significant features of the English Cabinet were that it was a party committee, and a secret committee—that is, a body that had no formal existence or authority, kept no records, and at which no outsiders were present.[4] However, the Cabinet's authority over legislation was almost unrestrained. The House of Commons, as distinct from the Government, had very little power.[5] Its right to refuse financial support to a Government was a constitutional figment. The value of Parliamentary questions was considerably circumscribed.[6] It was a training ground for public men, and the arena for electioneering purposes. No one could say that it represented even the majority of the electorate, except for a few months after an election. What there was, in fact, was a system of uncompromising party government.[7] In all these matters, Low's account of the state of affairs at the beginning of the century differs little from that of later writers in, say, the 1960s.

But perhaps the most interesting part of the book is the dismissal of Bagehot's fears, and the affirmation of the survival of deference.[8] In spite of the extension of the suffrage, no desire for sweeping innovations or revolutionary change had appeared.[9] The men of property, birth and superior education remained in the seats of power. Low added that 'Government in England is government by amateurs';[10] moreover, the widening of the vote, the practice of the secret ballot and the pressures of working lives, had meant that a smaller proportion of the electors took a real interest in affairs. He therefore was not without forebodings. Stability might be exposed to more searching tests

> Englishmen, for more than a hundred years, have been able to keep their politics clear of all the deeper issues that touch on ethics, on theology, on religious doctrine, on the relations of the individual to his own soul and to the visible and the spiritual

universe . . . This convenient simplicity may not be maintained.[11]

And he concludes with a disturbing vision:

> During the short London season, one may witness on any warm summer evening, a scene of strange significance. In front of some opulent mansion a long train of carriages and motor-cars will be in waiting after a fashionable entertainment. The opening doors reveal glimpses of sumptuous light and colour, the sparkle of gems on the bare shoulders of women, the shimmer of silk and velvet under the softened radiance of electric lamps. Outside, on the pavements, clustered about the carriages, so near that they could touch the departing guests with their hands, there will be a little crowd of quietly interested onlookers. Some of them are late workers, going homeward after their day's toil, poor, hard-wrought people, to whom a single glittering stone from one of the circlets uncovered before their eyes, might be worth the pain of a laborious year . . . Our modern wealth, kindlier, more self-restrained, less arrogant than in the past, yet lives under the curious gaze of a giant, always armed, and sometimes hungry.[12]

Sidney Low was a Conservative in party politics, and a strong supporter of the imperial power wing of that party. Like many others, however, he combined imperialist views with social reform principles in domestic politics.[13]

SOCIALIST IDEAS

As noted in Chapter 2, one expectation of both its friends and foes was that a democratic franchise would encourage demands for social and economic change. Thus the rise of socialist beliefs, and their eventual alliance with the labour movement, was the fulfilment of the hopes and fears of the previous generation. In his contribution to *Fabian Essays*[14] (1889) Sidney Webb argued that:

> The inevitable outcome of Democracy is the control by the

people themselves, not only of their own political organisation, but, through that, also of the main instruments of wealth production.

Just so: it was not only predictable but predicted. There was, Webb envisaged, an 'irresistible glide into collectivist Socialism.'[15] Not all socialists wanted democracy: indeed the term 'social democrat' was reserved at this time for those who believed in both. But Webb had no doubts. 'Every increase in the political power of the proletariat will most surely be used by them for their economic and social protection.'[16]

The Fabians were the moderate wing of the socialist movement and the one most committed to constitutional tactics. By permeation and gradualness, socialist aims would be achieved: the orthodox reforms of the liberal theory should be pressed forward, and then no other major political changes would be needed. Other socialists had less confidence. For some even in Britain socialism was not evolutionary but a matter of class struggle. Even so, it was noteworthy that the Social Democratic Federation began life in 1881 as the Democratic Federation, with adult suffrage as the first item in its programme. Under the leadership of the bizarre figure of H. M. Hyndman[17] (who always dressed formally in top hat and City attire) it developed a socialist programme of nationalisation of the means of production, and adopted a Marxist philosophy.

There was also the Independent Labour Party founded in 1893, with a collectivist programme, endeavouring to establish a Parliamentary presence. In 1900 unions and socialist bodies set up a Labour Representation Committee, the forerunner of the Labour Party itself. The tactics and objectives of these organisations varied: most engaged in electoral politics, socialist objectives were common, and their principles inevitably linked them with labour union activities. There were some indeed who would accept the need for a revolution of some sort. So there was plenty of evidence of socialist change in the air in the early part of the century. The control of the great parties in Parliament was still unquestioned, even after the 1906 Election, but the political proposition—that the next step from democracy was socialism—had become part of the debate. Many did not believe it and many did not welcome the prospect, but the question had forced itself into political life. It was an ancestor of themes discussed later, as collectivist arrival in Chapter 4, and as class conflict in Chapter 5.

It would be misleading to suggest that, at this stage, future socialism in a centralised and statist form was at all settled. There were already many socialisms.[18] Some of these pleaded for associational and voluntarist forms, and there were guild socialist and syndicalist movements in Britain at this time. Some indeed made the central state the object of attack in more radical fashion. *The Servile State*[19] (1912) by Hilaire Belloc was not only a contribution to the contemporary debate but the ancestor of movements for localised and community politics later in the century.

NEW RESEARCH

A new colour was added to the picture of politics by the arrival in the first decade of the century of the works that concerned themselves with political activity in a wider sense. Some of these were behaviouristic, and even ventured into empirical research. At any rate, they were more than the lively sketches of Bagehot or Low, and they were not legal texts.

The volumes of Moisei Ostrogorski's *Democracy and the Organisation of Political Parties*[20] (1902) are part of the foundations of political research. Volume I is concerned with British parties. It traces, exhaustively, the emergence of a new régime in the nineteenth century, leading to a more democratic constitution; it then describes, at length, the origins of political associations and party organisations. The crux of the thesis concerns the arrival of 'the Caucus'[21] (a small committee which meets to settle political matters before a larger meeting). These organisations—the Liberal Associations, the Conservative Associations and numerous ancillary bodies—could have decisive effects on the operations of the new politics.[22] The nominal intention was to make the government of the historic parties more democratic. Success was limited. The associations restricted the leadership somewhat and made it give attention to the views of party members, and it provided a political ladder for some to climb, and social access to those in power for others. But the new bodies overreached themselves: they did not have the abilities to cope with high politics, and they failed to provide the means of widespread political education. They allowed themselves to be managed

> This English middle class, which had played a glorious part . . . in the development of political spirit . . . now appeared in a new role, of an anything but lofty character; pretending to bow down before the masses, it let them say what they liked, allowed them the satisfaction of holding forth and of voting extravagant resolutions in the caucuses, provided that it was permitted to manage everything; and to cover its designs it developed the practise of wire-pulling.[23]

So Ostrogorski had a mixed verdict. Partly because they had to go to the trouble of managing the new system, the traditional party leaders had to change their techniques. But a great deal of deference survived, and the old order had not been overthrown. Internally, the local organisations had repelled moderate and independent-minded people and attracted enthusiasts: their great successes had been in organisation, agitation and electioneering.

Ostrogorski went on to study the situation in the political parties of the United States, and the general effect of his work was to stimulate the study of power within parties by other writers, and thereby the general thesis of inevitable oligarchy in organisations. In relation to British politics, the effect of Ostrogorski was to put in the forefront the fact of the party system. The era of the disciplined and nationwide party had arrived, and he had amply documented it. Thereafter political analysts could no longer leave these bodies on one side, as marginal to the constitution. Plainly the political system was dominated by them.

It may seem strange to put the two-volume treatise of A. L. Lowell *The Government of England*,[24] published in 1908, in this group. There are two justifications. First is its scope, which is wider than usual (though Lowell suggests that it is limited, having little about Scotland or Ireland). It includes extensive accounts of political parties (including socialist parties), non-party organisations outside of Parliament, local government, the educational system, the churches, the empire and the courts, and discusses their problems. Secondly there is its method. Since the forces he studied did not lie on the surface, he had to rely on conversations which he could use but not cite. In other words, he undertook research, no doubt unstructured but illuminating. Moreover, there were computations—notably about the increasingly disciplined nature of party behaviour in the Commons.[25]

Like Sidney Low, Lowell noticed a decline in the power of the Commons—it had lost both to the Cabinet and the electorate. Cabinets held power by virtue of electoral success: and this could only be achieved by public argument, and hence politicians made speeches from public platforms and sought publicity in the newspapers. The House was dependent on outside opinion— '. . . any strong popular sentiment is certain to find immediate expression there.'[26] Following Ostrogorski, Lowell recounts the history of the party organisations in both Liberal and Conservative parties and shows them to be reduced to electioneering bodies. 'Both are shams . . . the Conservative organisation is a transparent, and the Liberal an opaque, sham.'[27]

In his general reflections, Lowell remarks that Englishmen insist on their own lack of commercial enterprise, but believe that their government is the best in the world.[28] This government was still mainly in the hands of the upper classes, and their leadership was highly popular but it depended on retaining respect by unstained probity.[29] Upper-class society had a national, not a local character, and was brought together by education and social life. In Lowell's view, there was

> An almost complete absence of the passion for equality and the class jealousy so common in some other countries . . . the sentiment of deference . . . becomes stronger as the social scale descends.[30]

In Britain, a political candidate did not 'receive many rough buffets from men of less fastidious temperament.'[31] He admired the lack of local pressures for favours in Parliament, and in a chapter on the growth of paternalism he records the tinge of socialism and the growth of humanitarian sentiment.[32] He foresaw dangers, that of parties trying to procure support by conciliating large classes of voters, and of a division of parties into rich and poor fighting over the distribution of property, but they had certainly not come.[33] Changes in British government, he thought, would come slowly and the organism would constantly adjust itself to a new equilibrium.[34]

The thoroughness and the comprehensiveness of the work showed all the virtues of American scholarship. The judgments were detached, and somewhat complacent. It may be suspected that what the author most admired was the deference: he was, after all, a Lowell of Boston.

Graham Wallas was at one time a Fabian socialist, though he resigned from the Society in 1904, and he was the first Professor of Political Science at the London School of Economics. His best-known book is *Human Nature in Politics*,[35] published in 1908. It is a work of general theory, but nearly all its material related to the practice of British politics, and it was British attitudes to political life that it was intended to influence. It was clearly germane to the image people held of the political system in Britain.

Indeed, it was in this book that the word 'image' came into the political vocabulary—in discussing political parties, Wallas suggests that the name of a party when heard or seen calls up an 'image' that shades imperceptibly into a meaning.[36] The general purpose of the book was to attack the intellectualist or rationalist fallacy as it operated in politics—the belief that people made some mental assessment of the way in which their political actions would further ends which they support. In truth, Wallas argued

> Men often act in politics under the immediate stimulus of affection and instinct, and that affection and instinct may be directed towards political entities which are very different from those facts in the world around us which we can discover by deliberate observation and analysis.[37]

The 'entities' which attracted affection and instinct included nations and parties. He remained a convinced democrat, and avoided the conclusions which others drew from human irrationality—both the fears typical of Bagehot or Maine, and the elitism of French psychologists such as Le Bon and Tarde, who attributed the evils of crowd passions to democratic majorities. The pre-rational character of human impulses was, for Wallas, affected by memory and habit and thought.[38] He never abandoned the possibility of reform. His weaknesses lay in the lack of practical constructive proposals, and eventually in his tendency to mere exhortation.

In the final chapter of *Human Nature in Politics*, called 'Nationality and Humanity',[39] Wallas attacked the views of Mazzini, Bismarck and Milner, who thought that individuals could only find emotional fulfilment through political nationalism. He argued that such a view led to a sort of imperial egoism; and he feared (prophetically, in 1908) that the logical end of this was world conflict.[40]

Wallas marked (in Britain) an important change in political understanding. The hopes of some radical reformers were beginning to be seen as illusions; the achievement of full democracy did not end problems. Wallas began the process of trying to understand democratic political processes in a more sophisticated—perhaps more scientific—way. His work marked the change from regarding democracy as a crusading ideal to treating it as an actual phenomenon needing deep study both qualitative and quantitative.

BEFORE 1914

The picture of political reality in the eyes of most politicians up to the outbreak of the First World War was that painted by Bagehot, Dicey, Low and Lowell. Their rules, their constraints and their norms still prevailed. Nevertheless, it was widely perceived to be a system under stress. The issue of Home Rule for Ireland had become a constitutional issue and had taken ordinary procedures to their limit, and (in 1914) potentially beyond. There was also a socialist movement in which the potential of revolutionary doctrine was visible. It did not seem to flourish much in Britain: but the awareness of its spread on the continent made observers realise that things might change. Hence there had to be something specifically British to secure stability—a long tradition, perhaps; or the wide respect for the governing classes; or, as many thought, something positive in the way of social reform was necessary to maintain the political order.

For much of the nineteenth century the United States of America was regarded as a radical democracy, a dangerous or meritorious example according to the point of view. However, the British situation was very different. The United States had a prestigious written Constitution and a Supreme Court. Britain had neither. In the United States there was a fixed separation of powers and a federal system. In Britain on the other hand there was Parliamentary sovereignty and Cabinet government: the constitution could be changed and legislation determined by executive decision. So the potential of the 'will of the people' seemed greater—for good or ill—in Britain. Where the United States had constitutional restraints and rights, Britain had traditional deference. If that broke down—and there were radicals and socialists trying to break it down—then the comparative images of the two political systems would be transformed.

The other underlying fact about the political image of pre-1914 years was the perception that Britain was a leader in world civilisation—a 'first-rate nation' in Bagehot's phrase. For imperialists and others the maintenance of this position was a primary goal of political activity. Again, there was uncertainty. From the 1890s a concern for 'national efficiency'[41] had preoccupied politicians of all colours, from right to extreme left. Few would fail to argue that their particular proposals, whatever they were, would help to improve Britain's position as a great power. This problem became manifest reality in the post-1945 years, and will be to the fore in later chapters. But it was there in Edwardian Britain as a danger, a threat.

Nevertheless, there was still a feeling that Britain was a country which made its own way, that it could choose its own constitutional, or social, path. No one thought that it was seriously constrained by the pressure or hostility of the rest of the world. Thinking about the political system had certainly begun to include comparative studies—in both Bagehot and Dicey there were comparisons with others, to the detriment of the others—and certainly there might be something to learn. But British practices and policies could, by and large, be determined internally.

High politics, the politics conducted by Westminster politicians, London journalists and Whitehall civil servants, continued to flourish, and the outcome of controversy within these circles continued to be largely decisive. Both Low and Lowell noted the continued importance of Society (that is, high society) and its round of dinners and entertainments in linking and facilitating discussion between politicians and politically-minded people of all views, certainly including socialist intellectuals. Nevertheless, they were increasingly aware of the need for support. The rival elites now needed backing from voters, and hence from party caucuses in the provinces, from other organisations like trade unions or women campaigners, from tides of opinion which they no longer felt sure of managing. Managing low politics was an increasing problem in the practice of high politics. A divergence of political objective—that is, the criterion of progress—was discernible, in spite of cross-currents: there was a difference between those who thought primarily in terms of national power, and those who looked first for betterment of peoples' lives. Moreover, insofar as some of its advocates saw 'socialism' as a system-replacement for the existing 'capitalism', then the notion of a drastic break in continuity had edged its way into the political scenery.

The shock to the system, when it came, was not of this nature. War had been foreseen, indeed had been prepared for: but war so extensive, so widely spread, so prolonged, so costly and so bloody was in no one's expectations. How could it fail to affect the ideas people had about the way they were governed?

THE INTER-WAR YEARS

It goes without saying that the First World War made a deep impact on British politics. The Cabinet itself had been reformed: no longer an informal gathering, it had agenda, minutes, secretariat and staff. Moreover, a coalition Government had been in office, disturbing the customary rhythm of partly conflict. The military expansion had been accompanied by a great bureaucratic and budgetary expansion, setting precedents for future development. With the departure of Irish MPs from Westminster and the Government of Ireland Act of 1921 the problems of Ireland moved out of the limelight for fifty years. In 1918 the Representation of the People Act gave the vote to adult men and to women over thirty, and though other changes have followed, from this point the question of the franchise no longer held the centre of controversy. Indeed the war marked a great transformation in the status of 'democracy' in British political values. Henceforward all mainstream politicians and publicists insisted that democratic government was part of the traditional British way of life. Non-believers in democracy were reactionary or revolutionary heretics.

The great domestic transformation of the 1920s was the decline of the Liberal Party and the emergence of the Labour Party as the second party. There was no introduction of proportional representation and the two-party system restored itself in the 1930s, to the discomfort of the Liberals. The character of politics had been changed, however, by the convulsions and experience of the war itself, and by the victory of the Communists in the October Revolution in Russia. The existence of a Marxist socialist power in the world not only affected international politics, but affected the nature of left wing politics everywhere. Britain was no exception. The Communist Party of Great Britain was founded in 1920 from existing socialist groups,[42] but made few inroads on the growth of the Labour Party. Of course, the Labour Party itself was not a simple construction. In 1918 it adopted a written constitution and a state socialist ideology, though what this meant in programmatic terms has been a cause of division and confusion ever since. For fifty years from the 1920s however, the main division in British politics concerned the introduction, or avoidance, of some sort of socialistic programme.

Though there was a short General Strike in 1926 and anti-system parties emerged on the left and (eventually) right, the main currents of political activity remained parliamentary and electoral. The image of the system therefore remained 'constitutional'. In spite of the war, the shift in ideological balance, and the impact of economic depression, the outlines of the British system remained stable and recognisable. Many of the ideas of Bagehot, Dicey and Lowell were obviously becoming out of date, but they were not entirely useless: they were still the 'classic' authorities.

The classic liberal traditions of constitutional criticism and reformist proposals were carried on by Ramsay Muir, who had been professor of history at the University of Liverpool and at Manchester, in a book *How Britain is Governed* published in 1930.[43] Muir wrote on a wide range of historical and political subjects; he was a strong imperialist and eventually spent much of his time as a propagandist in the cause of the Liberal Party.[44]

Muir's analysis was strikingly original—not in that all his ideas were completely novel, but together they formed a fresh critique. Good Liberal that he was, he nevertheless echoed Victorian fears about democracy:

> Look at the faces of any crowd pouring out of a morning train on the way to work—some stupid, some harassed, some predatory, some vacuous, some trivial—and reflect that with them rests the determination of our destiny: however ardent a democrat you may be, you will have some moments of misgiving.[45]

However, Muir was not without hope and he had remedies. He began by noting that, as distinct from the American separation of powers, the essential principle in Britain was concentration of responsibility—that is Parliament and the Judiciary regulated and checked the action of 'the Government'.[46] But what was meant by 'the Government'?

> There are two main elements in 'the Government'. The first is what is commonly called 'the Ministry', and consists of the politicians . . . But there is another element, not less important, about which the political text-books and the historians have hitherto been strangely silent. This is the Permanent Civil Service.[47]

He goes on to discuss the position of the senior civil servants first, giving them pride of place over the Cabinet and Government. His views are not extreme; he was well aware that capable politicians could set new directions and exert considerable control. But in stressing the active governing role of the bureaucracy— in legislation, in administration and in finance—he went ahead of others

> The growth of the expert or professional element in the government of Britain has been quite as important in its effects upon the working of our system as the growth of democracy itself.[48]

Muir's remedy was clear, and anticipated by forty years the activities of later reformers. These new developments should be exposed to, '. . . an incessant stream of instructed criticism, and . . . brought under control on behalf of the nation . . . The machinery provided by the Constitution is Parliament.'[49] In particular, he proposed

> Some system of Standing Committees is the only means by which this need can be met . . . What is needed is a series of Committees, such as they have in America and in France, concerned with each of the main Departments of government, and empowered to call for papers and interrogate officials whenever necessary.[50]

Moreover 'All Orders and Regulations issued by the Departments under the powers given to them by Statute should be submitted to the Committees.'[51] Muir's reforming zeal extended to other aspects of the Constitution. He proposed a smaller Cabinet, to be brought about by consolidation and rationalisation of the great Departments,[52] largely on lines put forward by the Haldane Committee on the Machinery of Government in 1918.[53] He thought that the two-party system was breaking down, and could well be replaced—in practice probably by a three-party system.[54] He was strongly in favour of a reformed electoral system with proportional representation.[55] There should then be a reformed second chamber, mainly elected (again proportionately) by the House of Commons, with limited powers.[56] He recommended a system of devolution, to Scotland, Wales and regions of England.[57]

Muir also suggested a scheme of 'functional devolution' so that industry might be properly consulted. However, he was very critical of what he called 'control by organised interests outside of the Constitution.'[58] He had noticed, earlier than most others, the growing tendency of organisations of all types to try to influence candidates and Members of Parliament. What he most objected to, however, were attempts to exert direct influence on the Government, bypassing Parliament. He noted the activities of industry and trade unions in this matter with dismay

> All these attempts to dictate to or control the Government by organised special interests outside of the regular machinery of the constitution are, of course, exceedingly dangerous, whether they are made privately and behind the scenes, or openly and publicly.[59]

It was futile, however, to expect anything else, while Parliament remained weak. Only if Parliament really represented every substantial body of opinion could these extra-constitutional bodies be expected to withdraw.

Muir's analysis obviously contains much that is dated. It also contains much that lives, as criticism and as prophecy. His belief that a reformed Parliament and electoral system would stem the tides of change was optimistic. The bureaucracy and the interest group system grew after 1930 to sizes that not even he can have anticipated. Nevertheless his political grasp and foresight were impressive, and his work has been strangely neglected by subsequent authorities.

More famous, more widely read, and less critical was Ivor Jennings, an academic lawyer at the London School of Economics. Some of his criticisms of A. V. Dicey have already been noted. He preferred the term 'supremacy' to sovereignty of Parliament, because it was not associated with 'politico-theological dogmas'.[60] He suggested that in practice, and especially in matters relating to the Dominions, Parliament could effectively bind its successors; and in general he stressed the real limitations on Parliament's power. Yet in legal terms he was clear enough:

> Thus Parliament may remodel the British Constitution, prolong

it own life, legislate *ex post facto*, legalise illegalities, provide for individual cases, interfere with contracts, and authorise the seizure of property, give dictatorial powers to the Government, dissolve the United Kingdom or the British Empire, introduce communism or socialism or individualism or facism, entirely without legal restriction.[61]

Jennings's two great works were *Cabinet Government*[62] (1936) and *Parliament*[63] (1939). With the earlier *Law and the Constitution* (1933) they became standard reading for a generation or more. Most lawyers, administrators, and politicians looked upon them as authoritative works, and their contents were staple fare for students.

In *Cabinet Government*, Jennings stressed the central role of the Cabinet as the supreme directing authority, providing unity to the system. In the Cabinet 'and still more, out of it' the Prime Minister was in a position of special importance.[64] He was 'a sun around which planets revolve'. A general election was primarily an election of a Prime Minister.[65] Nevertheless, without party support a Prime Minister was nothing. 'The Prime Minister's power in office depends in part on his personality, in part on his personal prestige and in part upon his party support.'[66] Jennings described the new Cabinet secretariat, with agenda and minutes and all: the old informality had gone. The new trend to the creation of autonomous administrative bodies was noted. The doctrine of ministerial responsibility was expounded, as a current reality.

Jennings's method was to consult all memoirs, biographies, histories and other papers concerning the arrangements he described. It was intrinsically an historical method. Thus his works were more substantially researched than those of Bagehot or Low; and his major volumes were not strictly legal treatises like those of Dicey or Anson. Indeed, he seems not to have accepted the sharp distinction between law and politics fundamental to Dicey. To describe the practice, as he did, was to look for precedents and hence conventions: the result was a description of how government functions.[67]

Like Dicey, he placed great importance on public opinion as a determining factor. The constitution had four major principles:[68] it was democratic, parliamentary, monarchical and a Cabinet system. The fundamental aspect was democracy; and this implied free speech, free association and free elections.[69] The Commons and the Cabinet were instruments of democracy; all were subordinated to public opinion, which meant essentially opinion expressed at general elections. He stressed too the importance of the Opposition.[70] It is 'at once the alternative to the Government and a focus for the discontent of the people . . . If there be no Opposition there is no democracy'. Because there are regular elections, opinion has its influence at all times. 'Government, with us, is government by opinion . . .'[71]

In *Parliament* (1939) he noted that the real function of the Commons was to defend and criticise the Government, and the democratic principle underlay everything.[72] In later works, such as *The British Constitution* (1941) he continued to re-iterate his emphasis on public opinion.

> The truth is that 'the most common and least privileged of the people' have generally been conservative, while the 'conciliatory upper class' has sometimes been, on American standards, quite radical.[73]

The picture that emerged from Jennings's books was that of a stable well-ordered system, responsive to change but not overwhelmed by it. He had general sympathy with moderate socialist ideas, and supported the development of legislative and administrative means to enlarged state activity. The outcome was rather comfortable. Certainly his business was to describe, not to criticise or prophesy; even so, a high degree of satisfaction with his subject was apparent.

A very different attitude emerged from the writings of his friend and colleague, Harold Laski, in the 1930s.[74] Laski was the successor to Graham Wallas as Professor of Political Science at the London School of Economics, and achieved a youthful reputation as a theorist, advocating a version of pluralism in which authority in society was conceived as 'federal'—that is, it did not have a single source, and an individual might have allegiance to a number of associations, not to the state alone.[75] The institutional consequences of such a view were never clear, and in later years, Laski showed sympathy with Marxist, or neo-Marxist, concepts of political life.

The weakness and eventual collapse of the Labour Government of 1929–31 in the face of economic depression was a turning point for many observers. There were constitutional problems, for a new National Government (that is, a coalition) was created, under the existing Prime Minister, and installed in office some time before Parliament was dissolved. Laski responded with a pamphlet *The Crisis and the Constitution*[76] (1932). He emphasised the unusual procedures that attended the formation of the National Government. Indeed, there were no precedents for what happened; convention suggests that the Conservative leader should have taken over. Since precedent and convention, in the absence of laws were the stuff of the Constitution, what happened was unconstitutional. Laski was alarmed at the possibilities that would arise if a determined, fully socialist, Labour Party should achieve a majority

> All this inevitably makes one pause before accepting the traditional hypothesis that the mere conquest of a majority is a sure road to a Socialist victory. It is a necessary path to follow; but the recent emergency makes one wonder whether the serious problems will not begin when its end is reached.[77]

The Labour Party, in Laski's view, should prepare itself to meet a challenge at this point.

A more substantial critique appeared in *Democracy in Crisis*[78] published in 1933, based on lectures delivered in the United States in 1931. In this book he stated his conviction that below the surface of society there were symptoms of social convulsion.[79] Given this perception, the problems of the time were interpreted in dramatic terms of crisis, breakdown and revolution. The thesis was that events had shown that the economic system, capitalism, was no longer capable of progress or adaptation. In these circumstances its ruling class, the bourgeoisie, would abrogate normal political processes—-constitutionality and democracy—in order to preserve its power. The differences between the Conservative Party and the Labour Party were so great, and the transformation which the Labour Party intended was so fundamental, that it could not be brought about by normal processes. 'The rules of the game surely become different under these conditions.'[80]

> I believe, therefore, that the attainment of power by the Labour Party in the normal electoral fashion must result in a radical transformation of parliamentary government. Such an administration could not, if it sought to be effective, accept the present forms of its procedure. It would have to take vast powers, and legislate under them by ordinance and decree; it would have to suspend the classic formulae of normal opposition. If its policy met with peaceful acceptance, the continuance of parliamentary government would depend upon its possession of guarantees from the Conservative Party that its work of transformation would not be disrupted by repeal in the event of its defeat at the polls.[81]

These remarkable proposals, and others in the same vein have attracted much retrospective condemnation. Perhaps Laski was unduly alarmist, in the British context. However, exceptional political events were taking place: the world war and its aftermath, and the deepening depression in Britain; the revolutionary regime in the Soviet Union; and the rise of new totalitarian forces in Italy and (imminently) in Germany. It was not absurd to suggest that even insular Britain might find its traditions inadequate.

In his later work, *Parliamentary Government in England*[82] (1938) Laski presented a commentary rather than an informative description. The chief theme remained: the system had worked remarkably well, while it appeared to bring prosperity and national success. However, the party divide now embodied the class struggle, and their programmes were separated by an abyss. The 'Short Programme' of the Labour Party issued in Spring 1937, he suggested, gave no assurance to businessmen that the basic economic structure of society would be undisturbed. 'It is not . . . too much to say that it is an attempt deliberately to transform the purposes to which the State-power is devoted.'[83]

In the event, Laski misjudged the degree of conflict between the British parties, even in the 1930s. There was indeed a gulf between the attempts of the National Government to manage the economy and the 'practical socialism' which the Labour opposition adopted, but it was not an unbridgeable one. Of the economic analysis relevant to economic policy, Laski had no inkling. Soon, for this image of political reality, the events of the second world war were to present completely unexpected developments.

In any case, Laski's views were challenged by argument in the 1930s. A notable contribution was *The Essentials of Parliamentary Democracy*[84] (1937) by Reginald Bassett, a colleague of Laski's at the London School of Economics who supported the 'National Labour' party of Ramsay MacDonald. Bassett made the basic assumptions of the liberal democratic polity more explicit than before. If anything was fundamental in politics, it was 'the principle of the democratic method.' Agreement about the social order might or might not be there, but 'the agreement that *is* requisite is common agreement to seek agreement . . .'[85] But in the 1930s in Britain, Bassett agreed, there were dangers even at the procedural level.

THE 1939 PICTURE

If the scene in 1939 in British politics is compared with that of 1914, then a paradox presents itself. In many ways the system had proved remarkably stable, and observers noted the fact. In contrast with comparable structures in Europe, British institutions like Parliament, the Cabinet, the electoral system, the civil service, the monarchy and their constitutional relationships remained in good order and were held in high regard. On the other hand there were vast changes—the rise of the Labour Party had transformed the issues, the substance of what politics was about. The Empire had survived, but the expectations associated with imperialist ideas had dissolved, for the Dominions secured effective independence on policy matters, and the independence of India had become a live prospect. Most strikingly, alongside the stability, there was fear of disaster on the grand scale, in a way that had not been felt before 1914. In the preface to the first edition of *The British Constitution*, written in 1940, Ivor Jennings reflected that he had continued to write about it 'in complete disregard of almost daily prophecies from over the water that the next week was to see its overthrow.'[86] The contrast was apparent not only in 1940 but all through the 1930s.

The changes of the two decades can be seen as a response in high politics to major shifts in low politics. Certainly the readjustments of the party system followed what politicians thought were popular pressures. Nevertheless the high politics of London life continued: politicians, journalists and academic pundits mingled freely. The sway of high society no doubt began to decline somewhat, but the country-house weekend continued, supplemented by its pale imitation, the summer school. The Marxist interpretation, of course, divided politics into that of the working masses and that of the ruling bourgeoisie—low and high in a more significant sense. In retrospect what seems most interesting, however, is the way that this Marxist image invaded the world of high politics itself—not so much in Parliament, but in intellectual and journalistic circles. The ideological divide, insofar as it occurred, was not between classes. It flourished in high politics, within the élite itself.

Progress in general terms continued to mean betterment from invention and development, as it had for the Victorians. Economic politics was nevertheless about recovery from depression; there was not much room for euphoria. Continuity, so long the pride of British politics, was itself under question; some professed to see drastic change (by revolution or reaction) as a near possibility, and that for a few years was a new colour in the kaleidoscope.

4   A Theme, with Variations

The divisive passions always present in political systems had been exacerbated in Britain by the approach of the Second World War. The actual prosecution of the War, however, led to a degree of unity not seen before in the century. The unity was never complete, was always fragile, and was in some respects sporadic. Nevertheless the experiences of government during the war, and of the war itself, fostered an atmosphere of toleration in political life which lasted for thirty years after its conclusion. Any pretence of actual partisan unity broke down in 1945; and the extent of consensus which prevailed in subsequent years can easily be exaggerated. Yet the conflict and its international aftermath coloured the attitudes of more than a generation of active politicians.

The ideological configuration of the war was not as predicted beforehand, nor was it that of the cold war which has followed. True, the enemy powers were fascist in Europe and militaristic in Asia. For four years after 1941, however, the liberal-democratic allies in the west found themselves allied with the communist Soviet Union. In Britain itself, a coalition Government brought together Conservative, Labour, and Liberal politicians, under the leadership of Churchill. Conservatives thus fought the anti-fascist crusade and associated themselves with Soviet power. In the post-war years the Labour Government of Clement Attlee was among the prime organisers of the North Atlantic Treaty Organisation, the political and military alliance established to counteract Soviet power. Whatever the internal divisions of British politics, therefore, they did not stretch far, if measured on a world scale. The country did not tear itself apart.

Open political activity during the war was restrained by the existence of a coalition Government and of an electoral truce. The holding of a General Election was postponed until the end of hostilities in Europe, a vivid illustration of the extent of parliamentary sovereignty. However, parliamentary procedures and debates continued at all times, and political journalism flourished, limited mainly by paper rationing. There was even some political philosophy, and political novelists like George Orwell and Evelyn Waugh continued to publish. There was not, however, any major development in the vision of the system or any fresh constitutional analysis, the prime concerns of this study.

The major ideas of the post-war era can now be described.[1] In the rest of this chapter one main 'theme' will be defined and discussed, and some variations and developments explained. The following chapter distinguishes some other themes. Thus the straightforward chronological scheme of the previous chapters will be abandoned in favour of thematic grouping.

COLLECTIVIST ARRIVAL

The first interpretation to be discussed can be conveniently described as the arrival of collectivism. What arrived was not socialism, though it was at one time so perceived by some of its friends, and many of its enemies. It was certainly a form of fulfilment—of prophecies and of intentions. Those who saw events in this frame were the successors of the critics and reformers, of those who had sought to change an old order of things.

In brief, from this vantage point the main features to be seen were the wide responsibilities of government and the associated large apparatus, concerned with public administration and with policy-making. This growth, it was argued, was impelled by the electorate. It was what people wanted; and the political system, newly democratised, moved obediently to provide it.

There was a further widening in public perceptions of 'what politics was about'—most economic and social arrangments became legitimate matters of controversy. There was a series

of consequential changes, so familiar that it is almost
embarrassing to set them out. Political parties developed better
organisations and nationwide active memberships. The civil
service increased vastly in numbers and complexity, and so did
local administration. The proportion of the national income
taken by central government revenue rose from about 8 per
cent at the turn of the century to about 30 per cent in the fifties
and 33 per cent in the seventies.

Beyond the government service proper, a large number of
autonomous and independently constituted bodies later called
'quangos', were created or financed (or both) by the central
government. There was a system whereby the use of land was
controlled, and the development of the built environment was
subject to regulation. These expansions on the part of
government stimulated in turn the countervailing activities of
pressure groups: indeed most associations and interests found
themselves attempting to influence government in some way or
other.

This clutch of developments constituted the 'collectivism'
that arrived. However, the key to the theme now being
explored lay crucially not in the facts but in favourable
attitudes to the changes. Some people not merely welcomed
them but cried for more; others were less rapturous, but
certainly regarded them as necessary in the circumstances, and
hence politically desirable on balance. Not that even within this
broad class was everybody in favour of all the developments:
the definitional characteristic is merely that of general
approval.

It is relevant at this stage to note in passing two things. First,
similar changes occurred in other liberal-democratic
countries—British experience was not out of line. Secondly,
changes of scale and the growth of large organisations took
place in non-governmental sectors too. Indeed, the arrival of
giant business enterprises is just as significant a feature of the
twentieth century as government growth.

This theme was itself subject to a variety of interpretations.

The first variation of the theme was an interpretation best
described as simple socialism. It explained the developments as
the culmination of an historical process: the rise of the labour
'movement' and the defeat of *laissez-faire* ideas by socialist

critics. For the most naive, capitalism was going out and socialism was coming in. Even in less apocalyptic versions there was something dramatic about this view. Labour was a programmatic and an idealistic party: it was bringing about things long foreshadowed. The effective ideology was Fabian in that the process of change was strictly constitutional and brought about primarily by normal legislation; and the socialism was evolutionary and gradualistic.

In a sense therefore, the actual reforms were instrumental and practical, perhaps even temporary means to a distant purpose. The history and (more significantly) the mythology of the Labour Party made it necessary that programmed proposals should be carried out: there must be no diversion, no betrayal, no backsliding.

The political crisis forecast by Harold Laski in the 1930s did not occur. The Labour programme had little constitutional content, and was in part derived from the discussion of post-war plans (about full employment for example) in wartime. The other main source was the Labour Party's own political thinking of the 1930s, but in 1945 proposals for (say) nationalisation of basic industries seemed much less challenging, since the whole of industry and commerce had been subject to strict quantitative and price control during the war. Moreover, the Labour party and trade union leadership was at this time fully accepted in the political élite.

It need hardly be said that the Attlee Governments of 1945–51 were overtaken by problems in the economy and in foreign affairs that had not been foreseen. The world environment was still a turbulent one. For the evolutionary socialist, however, it was not merely a question of exchanging euphoria for reality. Even the most moderate of gradualists needed some notion of what should happen next. There was not merely a problem of devising a programme; there was a problem of political vision. What would 'further advances' look like?

Hence, in the 1950s and since, there has been a crisis in the socialist vision of the political system. In the main deep disputes and divisions in the party focussed on policy matters. But if, for all, socialism was a progressive phenomenon (that is, not a static or recurrent one) in the sense that there would be more and more of it, then a two-party alternation, with long periods out of office, could only be tolerable if the other party or parties were relatively passive. The traditional Labour view, for instance, required a gradual spread of public ownership in industry by nationalisation or other means. The revisionist school of socialists inspired by Anthony Crosland which flourished in the late 1950s and early 1960s rejected this emphasis and made much of the primacy of egalitarian values to be achieved by public provision of services. Did such a change of policy also change the image of the political system?

If Labour had come to regard itself as an ordinary party, sometimes in office and sometimes out, trying to govern according to its values, then things might have been different. But into the 1980s there was still hope that the 'forward march' could be resumed. Hence this simple socialist view survived: politics in Britain it claimed, was still essentially a conflict between those wanting to move onward and those resisting, delaying or confusing the issue. All else was distraction, nuisance or sideshow.

This picture was not visible to those of other parties or persuasions. Nevertheless a more pragmatic welcome to the collectivist trends was commonly found. It may be summarised thus: though individualism and *laissez-faire* had many desirable qualities, experience had shown that they also had grave defects. Moreover technological change and world events required large-scale organisation to cope. In these circumstances governmental guidance or intervention, often remedial and perhaps temporary was prudent.

So a second interpretation of collectivist arrival may be called the Conservative-pragmatic view. In fact Liberal writers were also involved. In post-1945 years however, the Conservative Party, while vigorously opposed to rash spendthrift socialism, was anxious to make it clear that it was not and had never been the party of *laissez-faire* (an opprobrium apparently reserved to nineteenth-century Liberals). No Conservative however moderate shared the egalitarian values of the socialists. Nevertheless they were prepared not only to accept most (not all) of the reforms of the Attlee Government, but also to initiate further expansions of state activity in industry, in education and in planning. There were certainly other philosophies in the Conservative party, and interludes when they prevailed. Nevertheless a sort of cautious collectivism generally held sway. Moreover this attitude was a common non-partisan or independent view, well to the fore in the civil service and the professions.

Both these views are conformable to wide visions of the place of Britain amid international developments—to ideas about the way the world was going. This matter became increasingly important, and will be much discussed later. It is time, however, to set out the dominant pictures of the post-war system in Britain.

It is important to stress that these pictures were of a 'system'. They were not merely constitutional descriptions. Constitutional discussion did not disappear, and has been recently resumed. But most political writers in the period thought of their work as something broader in conception.

The magisterial interpretation which dominates the period as Bagehot dominated the period before 1914, was that of Samuel H. Beer, in *Modern British Politics*, first published in 1965.[2] Beer was professor of Government at Harvard University and politically active in the United States in the Democratic Party. His exposition first analysed the five 'types of politics' which the British had experienced: Old Tory politics, Old Whig politics, Liberal politics, Radical politics, and eventually the politics of the 'Collectivist Age'. It then explored this current age in greater detail.

Fundamentally, Beer was concerned with a political culture, and he found the theory of representation the best way to exhibit the features of that culture. In his words, he looked first to 'the images and sentiments that function as operative ideas in a community' and then to the corresponding behaviour.[3]

In the period of collectivism, representation takes two forms; or it embodies two themes:

> The major theme of this Collectivist theory of representation is party government; its minor theme, functional representation.[4]

These two principles encapsulate the sytem of politics as it was seen and accepted in Britain: the main parties and others active in affairs recognised them as legitimate, as the right ways to carry on, and thus to an extent they became true descriptions. Though there were disputes about their forms, and there was some retained belief in the propriety of the liberal-individualist theory of representation, these collectivist ideas held sway.

The two themes need elaboration. 'Party government' implies the primacy of parties as such and their right to govern. Democratic choice is less a matter of electing individual representatives (who will then discuss and determine policies) as selecting a party which will form a government and then, by its majority, control Parliament. The collectivity—the party—is more significant than the individual MPs, and if it wins an election its right to govern is paramount. Beer assumed a two-party system and that the parties were competitive: hence they were engaged in a struggle for power which entailed a constant search for votes. Therein lay the democratic power of the people: they could choose between parties.[5] The concomitant for the parties themselves lay in emphasis on party unity and coherence.

The minor theme of functionalism was also present in the party system, in that major parties in practice embodied interests—of class, of status and hence of function in society. The importance of this theme lay in that it made the promotion of interest—the pursuit of sectional well-being—a recognised and legitimate political activity. Contrary to some suppositions of liberal theory,[6] it was not wrong to secure the welfare of the group by political means. Hence the way was clear for the advancement of pressure groups—they might be secondary to party rule, but their role was a proper part of the system. In practice, therefore, group pressure became familiar, normal and fully approved in political life.

The grounds on which the two parties found themselves supporting this dual system differed widely: the socialists' collectivism was a matter of class solidarity, that of the Tories was founded on respect for authority. There were of course, great divisions of philosophy and of policy between the parties. Nevertheless, Beer noted that respect for the system provided a high degree of consensus. These ideas had a powerful stabilising effect. And though he was not inclined to the flattery of Lowell nor the complacency of Jennings, Beer did not share the panic of Bagehot nor the forebodings of Laski. He concluded:

> Happy is the country in which consensus and conflict are ordered in a dialectic that makes of the political arena at once a market of interests and a forum for debate of fundamental moral concerns.[7]

One effect of this new model of the political system was to put different entities—'collectives'—at the centre of the stage. Instead of formal institutions, parties and pressure groups (the vehicles of ideas and interests) were given prominence. True, Government and Parliament and civil service remained, but their relations did not supply the essential dynamics of this model. Beer's picture was one of evolution and adaptation, not one of drastic change or crisis. The assimilation of interest-bargaining to the system was made easier by recall of the former constitution of the eighteenth century, in which such things were accepted.[8] There was no moral shock to existing order. Indeed, the assimilation of the new in Britain was made easier by the retention of institutions and procedures which soften the impact of change. There was, however, a serious moral conflict to be absorbed in Britain. In spite of consensus policies and procedures, the division between the Conservative and Labour parties reflected deep divisions of values.[9]

The new emphasis on parties and on pressure groups had been foreshadowed by previous research. In 1955 Robert T. McKenzie published *British Political Parties*.[10] McKenzie was a Canadian who became Professor of Sociology at the London School of Economics, and a famous political broadcaster. He redeveloped the deep study of internal party affairs in Britain, a tradition lost since Ostrogorski's work in 1902. The bulk of *British Political Parties* consisted of an historical account of the internal structure of the Conservative and Labour Parties, and of conflicts within them. In conclusion McKenzie raised the question of internal democracy. Following Michels[11] he argued that leaders retained most power whatever the constitution or ideology of the party might indicate. This analysis was in conflict with much of the Labour Party's self-image: McKenzie tried to show that it was not far removed from the practice of that party's reality.

McKenzie's study of parties led him to stress the common ground between them. In 1955 he thought 'The "agreement on fundamentals" is today very nearly as great as it has ever been in the modern history of British politics.'[12] This view contradicted the basic proposition of Harold Laski, and indeed much of the Labour Party's own claims for itself. It went much beyond the claims of S. H. Beer. In 1966 Beer and McKenzie debated their differences on the radio. Beer argued that in the post-war period the great moral issues were very important in British politics, underpinned by attitudes towards class. There was great conflict about how society was to be organised. The debate concluded:

> *Beer* Now to be sure . . . as these two parties came into conflict . . . they have to cope with the fact of governing, and they have to cope with the fact of winning elections. If they are evenly balanced, this may bring them very close together in actual policies. The different moral orientations of the parties nevertheless are very real . . .
> *McKenzie* I think 'orientations' I would accept; but I am not sure about 'moral orientations'.[13]

The other figures in this new composition were organised groups. Their political importance was discovered in Britain in the 1950s, shortly after a similar discovery in the United States. Again, Robert McKenzie provided the conventional understanding: pressure groups, he argued, provided a 'democratic enrichment'.[14] The existence of elections and parties was not enough for political activity. In order to influence action between elections, inside parties, at early stages of policy formation, and in complex ways, pressure groups were necessary to articulate opinions and perceived interests. They were supplementary, but nevertheless vital, not only to the public at large but to politicians and administrators who wanted to know what was afoot. In fact McKenzie held them to be more effective than parties:

> There can be no doubt that pressure groups, taken together, are a far more important channel of communication than

parties for the transmission of political ideas from the mass of the citizenry to their rulers.[15]

The exposure of pressure groups at work was carried on in the 1950s and early 1960s, by many other writers, including S. H. Beer, Harry Eckstein,[16] Allen Potter,[17] and many others. S. E. Finer, in *Anonymous Empire* (1958)[18] concluded with a plea for *More Light*: but on the whole the verdict was favourable. It should be emphasised that pressure groups were discovered, not invented—they already existed when these writers took up their pens, though in the 1960s they increased in numbers and prominence. So the growth was considered benign. Not only were they democratic, they were significant 'intermediate' institutions in mass society.[19] In wider terms, they also fitted conveniently into two more general political philosophies popular at this period—pluralism, which urged that freedom and democracy were sustained by a variety of organisations with a variety of values; and participative democracy, which required that a high proportion of the citizenry actually took part, in some way, in policy formation and governing processes. Pressure groups could be seen to be doing their bit towards these good causes.

It would be easy at this stage to conclude that analysis of the British political system was in a smug and self-congratulatory mood. The reader is reminded that this section of the exposition deals with those who found the expansion of government not unsatisfactory: for them the question was one of living with these new achievements. Even so, there were critics and reformers, within the stream, who questioned much that they found. Their contributions will be added to the picture shortly. But first another general theory must be added.

Anthony H. Birch was professor of politics at the University of Hull and of Exeter, and later at Victoria, British Columbia. His major work in this period was *Representative and Responsible Government*[20] published in 1964. He too sketched the history of Tory and Whig attitudes to representation, as the foundation of their constitutional ideals. These models were succeeded by a Liberal view of the constitution, of which Birch provides a classical summary:

This view, as it emerged in the second half of the last century, comprised four distinct but inter-related doctrines. First there was the theory of representation . . . the eventual aims of which were crudely expressed in the popular slogan 'one man one vote; one vote one value.' Second there was the doctrine of Parliamentary sovereignty, combined with the belief that in any conflict between the two Houses the views of the Commons ought to prevail . . . Third, Liberals insisted that ministers of the Crown were accountable to Parliament for their actions . . . Only in this way . . . could the political system provide for responsible as well as representative government . . . Fourth, Liberals attached great importance to certain legal principles that came to be known as 'the Rule of Law'.[21]

Taken together, these principles amounted to a theory of legitimate power.

Birch's particular contribution to theorising on the emerging polity lay in drawing attention to the parallel existence of another language of the Constitution: 'The other language is used by civil servants, the Speaker, Ministers of the Crown and opposition leaders who hope soon to become Ministers.'[22] The essence of this language lay in its emphasis on the continuing power and responsibility of the Government as the guardian of national well-being. In his textbook of 1967,[23] Birch explained that this 'Whitehall' view was a helpful guide to practice—in some ways better than the Liberal view. A great deal of executive activity in foreign affairs and defence is carried on independently of Parliament; but even in matters where legislation or approval is needed, the role of Parliament is essentially critical or persuasive. In Britain the Government not only controls a largely centralised administration, but determines financial matters and holds the initiative in all major policy matters. The executive is subject to other constraints in an open polity—from critics in the free media and from the need to secure the co-operation of other bodies. But these are hazards and problems; it is the duty and the prerogative of the Government (the inheritor of monarchical authority) to cope with them, just as its pre-democratic forerunners coped with the constraints of previous ages.

Whitehall language in spite of its realism had defects. It underestimated the importance of elections and the party changes they brought about, and indeed of public attention focussed on Parliament. Standing on its own it was not an adequate view of the British system. But, as Birch claimed, it was a necessary corrective. Both the Liberal view and the Whitehall view were necessary to understanding the true picture.[24]

This analysis did not secure the same popularity as Beer's. Perhaps it was not sufficiently coherent: the two views might have historical roots, and co-exist: but which was the better guide to action in the future? Perhaps 'Whitehall' was not a good title to this tradition: 'The tory vision' might have been better (though *not* 'Conservative vision'). Or, to anticipate the language of the 1980s, the expression 'strong state' picks up some of the essential spirit of the outlook. Whatever the name, however, experience in later decades has shown that Birch had sketched out one vital aspect of the British scene.

These two frameworks, of Beer and of Birch, constituted significant attempts to provide general images of the British system in its post-war manifestation. Published in the sixties, they held the scene for ten or twelve years; and they still provide the best political conspectuses of those times.

VARIATIONS

However, much further writing needs to be examined. The older tradition of constitutional writing was not dead (and there has been a later revival). The late 1940s saw the publication of Leopold Amery's *Thoughts on the Constitution* (1947)[25] based on the Chichele lectures at Oxford. Amery was a Conservative politician of note: indeed, there is some risk in including him in this section since if anyone of this period deserved the name of 'Old Tory' it was Amery. Indeed he commends Hearn's view that England still has the constitution 'under which the Confessor ruled and the Conqueror swore to obey.' (See above Chapter 2). In this book, nonetheless, he had reforms to put forward.

Amery's image of a traditional constitution is of interest. It was:

> based on the balance and adjustment between two elements each of independent and original authority, the Crown and the Nation. The Crown, as represented by the Government of the day, is throughout the active initiating and governing element; the Nation, as the guardian of the laws and customs of England, is entitled to refuse its consent to any changes in these without good reason given. The arena in which the two conduct their continuous conference or parley is Parliament.[26]

There is balance in this model but it is not a Whig balance; and the nation does not have the dominance it does in Liberal theory. Amery's proposed reforms however turn out to be not unfamiliar: procedural changes in the Commons; a committee system related to Departments; devolution to Scotland, Wales and regions; life peerages; a House of Industry. Within the executive he proposed a small Policy Cabinet.

In 1951 Harold Laski published his last work, a set of lectures delivered in Manchester, entitled *Reflections on the Constitution*.[27] It was in many ways a reply to Amery, and surprisingly cautious. For Laski, the nature of politics had been transformed by the rise of the Labour Party, a class party with an ideology far from that of other parties. In this view he retained his position of the 1930s to the end. Nevertheless, his institutional programme is moderate. He welcomed the idea of advisory committees in the Commons, but saw little merit in devolution, a House of Industry or a policy Cabinet.

These constitutional discussions were overtaken, for most of the period, by other approaches. Nevertheless, the mainstream understanding of politics in Britain was illuminated by various reform proposals in the fifties and sixties which can best be described as constitutional. The new emphasis on parties and groups did not exclude concern for the institutions in which they operated. As the period moved on, an increasingly depressing picture of these institutions was painted. For writers who accepted the collectivist spirit of the age it followed that it was the institutions that needed reform. The critics were usually dealing with particular situations, specific institutions, rather than drawing general outlines. Nevertheless, inferences about the larger whole must be made when studying a part.

An early post-war trend—now often forgotten—was to give greater weight to the study of 'government' itself. If the apparatus had expanded so much, then it needed investigation; and, indeed, understanding of the political system itself could not be sensibly sustained if what went on within the apparatus was not analysed. About this time the term 'public sector' came into use, but there was not in fact any unified monolith firmly under the control of the central departments. In fact, what was being created was a complex web of relationships, with many mixtures of control and autonomy, regulation and independence.

In the 1950s, W. A. Robson, Wilfrid Harrison, K. C. Wheare, and D. N. Chester all published works designed to further this sort of understanding.[28] In 1957 W. J. M. Mackenzie and J. W. Grove published *Central Administration in Britain*,[29] a textbook which constituted a classic of this type of work. There was plenty of information and there was a clear, indeed vivid portrait of the whole complex structure: but it was not dynamic and it was scarcely conceptual, let alone theoretical.

It would be hard to say that this movement made great impact on the public vision. For one thing, the descriptive nature of the books made them rapidly out of date. Not until much later in the period was much administrative theory written: and little of that has had political consequences. The translation of this approach into 'policy making' has had more success, and attention will be given to it later.

Much more in the public eye has been the study of elections. Pioneered at Oxford in 1945, there has followed a long series of works analysing general elections in Britain.[30] In the main these have served to establish a reliable record of campaigns. More searching enquiries began at Greenwich in 1950, though results were not published until 1956 in *How People Vote*[31] by M. Benney, A. P. Gray and R. H. Pear. One inference from this early research was that—as Graham Wallas had argued—human nature in politics was non-rational. People did not vote according to their policy preferences: or, at least, a proportion of them voted for parties with whose policies they did not agree. Indeed as the editor of the volume put it: 'Those whose *political* education is highest often show both the highest degree of loyalty to the party, *and* the greatest disagreement with the party's programme.'[32] The debate on this matter was not a particularly British concern, for the same phenomenon was observed elsewhere. However, it is not necessarily irrational to vote on grounds other than policy preference—class sympathy or family tradition are themselves reasons.

In the 1950s and 1960s much more sophisticated analyses of voting behaviour appeared. Much of this work merely reflected the current trends in electoral favour. Thus the Conservative victories of the 1950s were accompanied by the theory of 'embourgoisement' of the electorate, but when Labour won elections in the 1960s doubt was cast on the effect on voting of the social changes. Even more formidable studies were made in the 1960s and 1970s—*Political Change in Britain* by D. E. Butler and D. Stokes[33] (1969) and *Decade of Dealignment*[34] by Ivor Crewe and Bo Sarlvik (1983). The work of Butler and Stokes drew attention to the importance of family tradition and to demographic factors. The research at the University of Essex was able to follow the growing dealignment of the electorate, both in its partisan loyalties and its class identification.

Certainly for the general image of the system, special interest lay in findings about class voting. The electors might not be much influenced by policies, but they were influenced by their class membership:

> Class is the basis of British party politics; all else is embellishment and detail.[35]

declared Peter Pulzer in 1967. If this was the case, then something might be said about the fears of Bagehot, the illusions of Low and Lowell, and the hopes of socialists like Webb and Laski. Class *difference* had become the basis of political conflict—nevertheless the system could contain and absorb it. Class-based parties could, it seemed, operate within the norms and understandings of British constitutional politics. Nevertheless, even in the forties and fifties, the class basis of voting was not simple. Some middle-class people voted Labour, and some of them became leaders of that party. More significantly, something around a third of the working class (a term of varying definitions) voted Conservative. This fraction of the electorate, the working-class Tories, received considerable research attention, since it was clearly of major importance to the presumed balance of parties in the system.

In the 1960s and more vividly in the 1970s and 80s, this vision of class voting all but disappeared. Studies showed that the Conservatives could get about as large a proportion of working class votes as Labour. Class loyalty it was alleged, was no stronger than partisan loyalty.[36]

This realisation could have several consequences for the image of the system. One possibility might be that a healthy opinion-based debate was emerging. Another interpretation was that there was a growing disenchantment with the system itself. If this were so, then some might welcome the abstention from politics and public affairs as a turn to self-reliant life expectations. Others might look elsewhere than conventional politics for the arena in which the real irreducible class conflict manifested itself (and so beyond the 'collectivist arrival' theme). On the whole the early voting research provided a clear view of this part of the polity; the effect of later, and on the whole better research, has been to make the image blurred and confused. There were attempts to restore the relevance of class to voting behaviour, by redefining 'class', and so some of the old arguments about the importance of social position could be restored in new forms; but no one could make things simple again.[37]

It is not the purpose of this book to appraise this body of knowledge. What is of concern is its effect on political beliefs about the nature of the system. Various possibilities may be suggested.

(a) If the greater understanding could be 'applied' by political leaders and their advisers, they would have new advantages. They remained in competition with one another, but the management of electoral strategy was more professional and less instinctive. 'High politics' was still, in part, about the control of 'low politics'. Thus the system was susceptible to elite manipulation.

(b) However if political leaders came to believe that elections were determined by 'objective' factors, rational or non-rational, they might also feel that policy could be safely distanced from electoral pressure. Even if policies had *some* effect on voting, one or two unpopular policies could be carried—because the rising generation was inclined to vote Labour anyway, for example, or because house-owners living in the south are likely to vote Conservative anyway.

(c) Therefore two contradictory effects on the political operations could and did follow. At first it seemed that what the parties had to do was to adapt to a changing society, and engage in a sort of rival tailoring service, so that they could fit the (known) electoral factors. On the other hand, given the importance of image and of the existing Government's state of popularity, there might be many ways to win. Hence diverse ideological paths might be sought, and given the vagaries of the first-past-the-post electoral system, neither moderation nor extremism had any particular advantage.

Whether these are genuine inferences from scholarly works may be doubted. The high-water mark of this sort of reasoning was reached in the early 1960s. Some argued that since British Prime Ministers had, within limits, the right to choose the date of the Election, and that they could manage the economy and read the opinion polls, then Governments were unlikely ever to be defeated.[38] This facile theory was soon disproved by events. Nevertheless it is true that electoral and other research into political beliefs has provided an ambience of professionalism and sophistication to political tactics. Moreover, Parliament was not the only sounding-board any more, and so its reactions could be discounted. While active politicians believed they had to seek a middle ground in order to win, the theories of Jennings, Beer and McKenzie held; but if these beliefs were abandoned (wisely or unwisely) then the tendency to reciprocal moderation would be lost.

Opinion research, not necessarily connected with elections, obliged observers to take a less than heroic view of political mandates. It became possible to know the opinion of people on matters of Government policy and action with reasonable credibility. The right of a Government (and of its parliamentary majority) to govern could no longer plausibly refer to popular support for particular actions, since this was often shown to be lacking. Such information did not, of course, affect short-run policy very much, but it added to the sophistication of the electoral strategists.

Within political studies itself, however, more fundamental changes were taking place. The study of parties, pressure groups and elections could be regarded as an extension of the existing institutional tradition. Under American influence, however, some political scientists attempted a shift in the methodological orientation. Instead of philosophising about the nature of the polity, or examining the implications of constitutional rules and practice, what should be done was to observe actual political behaviour. This was of course, another stage in what is probably an infinite quest in search of reality. Bagehot and Dicey, it will be remembered, both claimed to be realistic—rejecting paper descriptions, or discerning the actual legal constitution, and discovering the real political sovereign.

Two well-known applications of this approach to British politics will serve as examples. In 1963 Jean Blondel published *Voters, Parties and Leaders*[39] which emphasised the social basis of political activity, and his analysis proceeded from social structure through electors, politicians, parties and interest groups to bureaucracy and 'the web of government' at the end. Richard Rose's textbook *Politics in England*[40] (first edition 1965) was more explicit. This book, at least in its first edition, put forward a distinct view of the nature of the British polity, in that the exposition was made to fit a standard pattern, allegedly appropriate to all political systems. This derived from Gabriel Almond's 'Functional Approach to Comparative Politics'.[41] Rose claimed that

> Emphasizing processes and functions common to all societies, such as political communication, has the advantage of leaving open to empirical investigation the contribution that various political and social institutions make to this process.[42]

Such an approach would show what to leave out as well as what to put in.

> Furthermore, by concentrating attention on processes common to a wide range of political systems from England to Ethiopia, comparisons are possible across national boundaries, across continents and across cultures.[43]

Rose followed Almond's categories[44] very broadly, beginning with the political setting, political culture and socialisation, and concluding with the policy processes and the means of legitimation. In later editions Rose modified his pattern of exposition, giving greater prominence for instance to the 'Constitution of the Crown', that is, Whitehall, Parliament and the Law.

In general, however, these approaches put less emphasis on the activity of governing and more on the activities by which the pre-governing process is sustained. This is in marked contrast not only to the traditional balance of Bagehot, Dicey, Jennings, Laski or Amery but also to the attempt in the 1950s to stress the work of government itself as crucial to the understanding of politics to an era of high state activity.

The general implication of behaviourist or functionalist studies, for the interpretations reviewed in this book, is therefore that the British polity is to be looked at (like other systems) as a variant within an archetypal 'political system', or small set of systems. All systems will of course have some different features, and it is the business of research to delineate these differences. Comparative study is therefore a prime method. This does not exclude other methods, but there is a difference in emphasis from the attempts to explore the evolution of tradition, or to infer principles from practice, the methods of Bagehot, Dicey, Low, Muir, Jennings, Laski, Beer and Birch. No one would accuse behaviourists, in Britain, of holding very restrictive methodological positions or being unreceptive to other work. Moreover, their writings do not place them outside the mainstream school of thought. Perhaps behaviourists *must* accept the conventional wisdom, as at any rate a prime determinant of the order of things. Whatever the importance of this change for political research, its influence on the picture of the system was gradual and pervasive, and not startling.

One school of writing in the period was marked by an explicit notion of the nature of the British system. This was the movement for Parliamentary reform, particularly of the House of Commons. There was indeed a Study of Parliament Group active since 1964 in promoting serious research, and much of the contemporary understanding of Parliament emanates from research associated with this Group. Its crowning achievement in terms of scholarship is *The House of Commons in the Twentieth Century*[45] (1979) edited by S. A. Walkland.

The reform campaign, which ran alongside this research, really got under way in the 1960s. A foundation document was an article, much reprinted, by A. H. Hanson, 'The Purpose of Parliament'[46] published in 1964. This endorsed strongly the view that the role of Parliament was 'advisory' in nature—not to limit or restrict the actions of Government, but to influence them. The most famous reform programme appeared in Bernard Crick's *The Reform of Parliament*[47] in 1964. He stated at the outset:

> The need for strong government can be taken for granted. But strong government needs strong opposition both if it is to be free government and if it is, in the long run, to be efficient and effective . . .[48] There is no incompatibility between strong government and strong opposition. Changing circumstances demand both.[49] [And later in the book] Parliamentary control of the executive—rightly conceived—is not the enemy of effective and strong government, but its primary condition.[50]

This view of the actual work of Parliament is, of course, the classic one, well grounded in much liberal theory as well as collectivist ideas. Both John Stuart Mill and W. E. Gladstone can be quoted in its support. However, the view that their respective 'strengths' were not reciprocal (that is, that power is not a zero-sum relationship) is more significant. It involved devising means of reform that would fit this principle. In practice the central feature of the programme has been the development of Select Committees in the House of Commons,[51] which scrutinise executive activities of Government, usually after they have taken place. This system preserves executive authority intact, but enables Parliament to expose, examine, and criticise the policies and actions of Government in some detail. There is a large literature on this subject, and it is not germane to this book to review it.

The point is that such an approach to reform accepts wholeheartedly the beliefs of the collectivist age. The intention was to make Parliament more efficient and more effective at doing what it should do. Bagehot's description of Parliament's functions was adequate.[52] They should be done better—in ways made necessary by big government. The reform of Parliament was about Parliament, not about the political system. Stuart Walkland, a persistent critic of this approach, complained that without wider changes, mere parliamentary reform could not be effective.[53]

Parliamentary reform did include changes besides Select Committees, and in fact there has been some effect on the system. Making Parliament better informed has carried with it the notion of a more dedicated body of MPs. Governments are compelled to give even more attention to Parliament, as a matter of routine. Moreover, in the 1970s at any rate it was discovered that the control of parties over their own MPs (through the Whips) was not as close and well-disciplined as had been believed.[54] Such developments made an impact on the balance of forces within the political system. Nevertheless they do not compel a transformed model to be created: a partially retouched picture is sufficient.

In 1967 A. H. Birch emphasised that the 'real dichotomy in British politics is between the government and the Opposition, not between government and Parliament.'[55] Developments since then have done something to soften the force and clarity of this proposition, but not enough to reverse the priority. The opposite is not yet true.

Another much-discussed topic in the period was the power of the Prime Minister. This took the form principally, of a controversy about the proper description of the situation, and turned on rival analyses of the existing state of affairs. Its relation to the general image of the collectivist age was derivative. The greater power of the Prime Minister, was the result, so it was claimed, partly of institutional changes but also of the nature of political business in government, in the new circumstances of collectivism.

The most scholarly version was put forward by John Mackintosh in *The British Cabinet*[56] (first edition 1962).

While British government in the latter half of the nineteenth century can be described simply as Cabinet government, such a description would be misleading today. Now the country is governed by the Prime Minister who leads, co-ordinates and maintains a series of Ministers all of whom are advised and backed by the Civil Service.[57]

Decisions are taken in various ways, but 'The Cabinet holds the central position because, though it does not often initiate policy or govern in that sense, most decisions pass through it.'[58] This argument aroused much controversy and criticism. However Mackintosh maintained his view, the key proposition for this book being his conclusion to the second edition: 'The politics of the 1960s . . . have led contemporary British Government to be described as Prime Ministerial rather than Cabinet Government.'[59]

This revelation was taken up by Richard Crossman and presented in an exaggerated form in his introduction to Bagehot's *English Constitution*, where he suggested that the Cabinet had become a dignified rather than an efficient part of the system.[60] Nothing in Mackintosh's or other informed accounts justified this relegation.

The 'Prime Ministerial' thesis was not itself reformist—though for some it might have implied that collegiate Cabinet power *ought* to be restored; for others, including Crossman, it suggested that the Prime Minister ought to have a large staff or a Department as a base. The interest in the context of this book lies in the theoretical variation attempted—from Cabinet government, a view ascribed to Bagehot but crystallised by Jennings, to something better called Prime Ministerial government. Three observations may be made (i) a great deal depended on the interpretation put on these phrases by the various controversialists; a good measure of cross-purpose and overlap was apparent; (ii) the controversy stemmed from the Prime Ministership of Harold Macmillan, and the problem lay in trying to interpret the enigmatic Harold Wilson; the arrival of Margaret Thatcher in office put a very different complexion on the matter; (iii) the various views all accepted the 'collectivist arrival' interpretation of the needs of big government and contemporary democracy.

It may be noted that in these models there is very little place for non-central government. At the outset indeed British politics was largely perceived as homogeneous: parties, interests, most government policies were nationwide. Socially, 'Britain is probably the most homogeneous of all industrial countries'[61] wrote Jean Blondel in 1963. When people voted in local elections, they followed national trends. In fact the post-war period saw the maturing of a long compaign for local government reform—new structures for London (1963) and the rest of the country (1972) were put into operation. In the late 1960s and 1970s even more dramatic changes were planned. Following a Royal Commission on the Constitution,[62] which in fact confined itself to the question of devolution, Bills were passed by Parliament offering measures of self-rule to Wales and Scotland. In Scotland a new Assembly was envisaged. These measures failed to gain enough support in referendums held in 1979. The topic of territorial government and politics, however, gained a new prominence. More significant than either was the breakdown of the arrangements for governing Northern Ireland after 1968, and the eventual installation of 'direct rule' from London. These changes could not fail to make an impact on the image, if only by generating a large academic literature.[63] Things could never be the same again.

All these changes, and proposed changes, however, were managed through the central institutions of Whitehall and Westminster. The proposed Scottish Assembly, and any possible legislatures in Northern Ireland, would be set up by Act of the United Kingdom Parliament at Westminster. The unitary state did not propose to abdicate.

If these trends had developed, then a substantial revision of the picture of a single British political unit might have been necessary. In the 1980s however, the Conservative government concentrated on central control of local government, abolished metropolitan counties, and showed no interest in devolution. The local government measures aroused much resentment, and the notion that localities should have a constitutionally recognised place in the system was put forward. Nevertheless, in the event and in general, it is necessary to say that few of the models of the British polity—in this theme or in the others—made territorial diversity a major feature, except in the 1970s.

THE THEME'S DEVELOPMENT

A summing-up of this theme—that of collectivist arrival—can now be attempted. The arrangements of British politics were seen to be the result of modifications of an inherited system, these changes being primarily brought about by the mass electorate and the scale of governmental activity. Conflict was structured by the vigour of a two-party system, party rule being the legitimate form of power. The ideas involved (such as socialist egalitarianism and conservative paternal authority) were philosophically wide apart but within the polity they could co-habit, because there were social pressures, electoral necessities, and an intellectual ambience that encouraged political toleration.

This traditional order was reinforced by the shared experience of the second world war and its international aftermath, and by the permeation of new-liberal ideas (such as Keynesian economics, social insurance and health services, planning controls, educational expansion, regional policies, and agricultural subsidies). These policies brought with them increased interest-group activity. The great political institutions were increasingly seen as frameworks in which these motivating forces operated, rather than prime movers themselves; they were often regarded as ripe for reform.

The extent of survival was remarkable: the descriptions of the British system at the beginning of the century contained much the same set of characters as the post-1945 accounts—grown fat and immensely complicated, but still recognisable. Only the great interest groups and 'quango' institutions were real twentieth-century developments. The image created by this school of thought was one of an undesigned system, proud of its own merits, coping bravely by its flexibility, and needing more and more accretions to make it work. Nevertheless reform and development would preserve an essential continuity. The 1960s saw attempts at many such incremental institutional reforms.

The three questions which were asked of the various models in previous chapters may be raised again. How did the 'collectivist arrival' school of thought treat the relation between high politics and low politics? It was an age of mass franchise. The great analysts—Beer, Birch, Finer, McKenzie, Crick—tended to assume elite competition and the need for interests to be pressed at the governing levels. Low politics were still constraints, factors to be reckoned with, problems to be managed; though in the 1960s there re-emerged briefly the participatory dream of democracy everywhere.

The period was marked by a narrowing of the concept of progress. In the post-war years the need for economic growth took over as the paramount objective, and this was reflected in political writings. The cause of the Empire disappeared, and had departed from the books before the colonies became independent: no one was interested in setting bounds any wider. Even on the left schemes for solving economic problems proliferated; democracy and social justice were the means, the preconditions, of faster growth. Towards the end of the period too there was a change in the attitude to reform. Gradualism was less in favour; radicalism was the recommendation on left, right and centre. Apart from the sectarian groups of the Trotskyist left, no one was looking for actual revolution. In the heated atmosphere of the mid-1970s crisis, however, there were occasional speculations about a military coup. But the real development was talk about fundamental change in the political system—a written constitution, electoral reform, devolution and other measures began to be advocated not as piecemeal advances, but as means to securing sharp and drastic change in the *political* system. This change in mood was in practice reflected in the style of the Conservative government after 1979, but radicalism, of some sort, was regarded with favour in most quarters, even the political centre.

The dominance of this interpretation (collectivist arrival) weakened drastically in the 1970s. Nevertheless there were responses to the crisis of those times that lay within this view of

British politics. One conspicuous change to the image presented was the new awareness of the United Kingdom as a complex of nationalities. Previous writers, even of classic stature, refer to England as if it were the whole: Bagehot's book is called *The English Constitution*. Nothing much disturbed this innocence—even Irish independence—until the late 1960s. The intellectual change was impelled by the real world: by trouble in Northern Ireland, by nationalist pressure in Wales and Scotland, and by proposals for devolution. Paradoxically the impact so far has been more clear in the literature and the image than in practical affairs. Homogeneity is no longer assumed. When Richard Rose wrote *Politics in England* the title meant what it said; when he wrote *Understanding the United Kingdom* the different range is made explicit.

The picture of a polity developing within its own traditions began to change in the 1960s, and in the 1970s it underwent severe crisis. The 1960s were years of economic frustration, and were characterised as a 'decade of disillusion' in other respects.[64] For a time indeed, it seemed possible that new institutions of political importance might emerge. In 1962 the Conservative government established a National Economic Development Council to promote economic growth; and in succeeding years institutions (first the National Incomes Commission, and then the National Board for Prices and Incomes) were created to deal with incomes policies. These were crucial matters in national politics, not specialist side issues.[65]

In the event they did not prosper, and that contributed to the disillusion. But their example, and the persistence of the habits of thought behind them, led observers to attach weight to the British fondness for tripartism—that is, the operation of bodies (councils, committees, quangos) based on three main constituents: the Government, business representatives, and trade unionists.[66] In many cases of course, the set-up was more complex than that. But the simple model presented itself as some sort of ideal—as a proper way to manage affairs.

Its ethic was one of consultation leading to consensus. It was obviously readily derived from the assumptions of the 'collectivist age', in particular that of Beer's minor theme, the legitimate representation of interests. When the crisis broke in the 1970s it came in for much vilification, and its weaknesses were exposed. But even before then such institutions attracted suspicion, for obvious reasons, from those who saw them as challenging their own power—Members of Parliament, the Government and the civil service. Potentially, they heralded a distinctly new political system.

Such a possible development fell within the definition of this theme, collectivist arrival, because its progenitors welcomed or accepted the need for large government activity. It was still an extension of what had gone before. Nevertheless, another concept emerged (or was revived)—corporatism.

A moderate version of the corporatist thesis was put forward by Keith Middlemas, in *Politics in Industrial Society*[67] (1979). He suggested that since the First World War, or before, the Government had found it necessary to treat, at the highest level, with independent forces in the economy. Often these were trade unions, sometimes employers. In any case, the constitutional power of the Government (including its parliamentary majority and its control of the executive machine) was irrelevant.

The realities of the situation required a deal, a bargain. The general motive, according to Middlemas, was crisis avoidance. The circumstances of such negotiations were occasional to begin with, but were becoming more frequent. This practice induced a *corporate bias* into the political system—certain organisations had more influence than the rest of the community and prudent rulers would accept this fact.[68]

In contrast to these cool analyses a more thoroughgoing and alarming message appeared in an article in 1974 by R. E. Pahl and J. Winkler. In 'The Coming Corporatism'[69] they forecast the establishment of a full corporatist system in Britain by 1980. Corporatism, seen as 'fascism with a human face', was a system of state control of (mainly) privately-owned firms. As such it was an alternative system to either capitalism or socialism. The state steered industry by four values. *Order* would eliminate the anarchy of market insecurity, especially the labour market; *Unity* would encourage co-operation in overcoming crises; *Nationalism* would encourage effort, to keep up with others; and *Success* would mean the achievement of state objectives, such as cutting inflation and increasing growth. It sounded exciting.

This was a prophecy, not a description. In practice the tripartite structures in which corporatism might flourish were in trouble. The NEDC was no longer in the forefront of politics. In the 1970s the Labour Government established a liaison committee to hold regular discussions with leaders of the Trades Union Congress, about economic, industrial and employment matters, including pay, under the so-called Social Contract arrangements. It was bilateral, not tripartite. This was the peak of corporate bias, however, rather than a fully-fledged corporatist structure. In 1980 very different policies were in operation.

Nonetheless, the existence of corporatist practices has persisted. Less dramatic but soundly based research shows that at many levels the integration of public authorities with private bodies flourishes. The Government gets its way through the operations of the independent interest group in return for allowing it a due measure of influence on policy.

Wyn Grant, a persistent critic of peak-level tripartite forms of corporatism in Britain, nevertheless argues that corporatist arrangements (properly understood) flourish at the middle level, between particular Government bodies and particular interest groups, such as in the dairy industry. Corporatism is more than pressure-group pluralism. It refers to

> A process of interest intermediation which involves the negotiation of policy between state agencies and interest organisations . . . where the policy agreements are implemented through the collaboration of the interest organisations and their willingness and ability to secure the compliance of their members.[70]

The right to negotiate and the ability to comply are the essentials.

The question is whether this form of corporatism, or meso-corporatism, can occupy the centre of the stage in a vision of the British political system. The care and rigour of the enquiry seem to have taken the phenomenon into the sidelines.

Perhaps an associated thesis may elucidate the problem. In

1979 Jeremy Richardson and Grant Jordan published *Governing under Pressure*,[71] subtitled 'the policy process in a post-parliamentary democracy'. This term implied that the days of parliamentary government had passed, and indeed that the fears of the parliamentary revivialists had come about. The method of Richardson and Jordan was to discuss the findings of various studies of policy-making. If the history of established policies was examined, how did these policies come to be adopted? They concluded that the liberal image of policy origins, or policy impetus from the popular level was very misleading. Even Parliament and parties were but particular factors among many

> The familiar framework for studying policies—examining legislative behaviour, political parties, elections— inadequately explains how key issues are managed. We see the current policy style as the balancing of group pressures. It may once have been legitimate to see the role of groups as simply articulating demands to be 'processed' in the legislative/ governmental machine . . . a symbiotic relationship between groups and government has developed . . .[72]

Thus by examining the development of policies from inception to implementation a new image of the polity emerged, one in which old institutions and forces were seen to be interacting. There were different 'policy styles' in different parts of the system. 'Groups', which were the agents of pressure, were defined widely to include bodies within the Government and administration, as well as the 'associations' of citizens familiar in a previous pressure-group theory. The book discussed both the policy framework and the processes which shaped policy. It concluded:

> If our book has achieved anything, we hope it has at least convinced the reader that for . . . Britain . . . the traditional model of Cabinet and parliamentary government is a travesty of reality . . . Politics, in a sense, has gone underground.[73] . . . We should . . . beware of any notions that we can return to a 'purer' age. Governments have always struck bargains with barons.[74]

Readers will no doubt contrast this image not only with those created by Bagehot and Dicey, but with those of Beer and Birch. Compared with Beer, there was less stress on 'party government'—the minor theme (functional representation) had taken over. Parties were there of course, but they too were permeated by group influences. And those who talked the 'Whitehall language' described by Birch needed to look not only at the dependence of the central power on other 'barons' but to observe the fragmentation within that centre.

The book has an obvious relation to corporatist arguments, though the view it presented fell short of the more explicit and precise corporatist theses. The key notion was of a 'symbiotic relationship'. It also showed how the study of policy-making (as distinct from old-style public administration) could make an impact on the understanding of a political system—it provided generality and it developed concepts. A more recent study by Brian Hogwood, *From Crisis to Complacency?*[75] analysed British policy-making as a stage-by-stage process, from 'setting the agenda' to implementation and evaluation of the policy, and illustrated the same point.

One major change in the image of the polity brought about by the adoption of the policy-making viewpoint lay in the role of the civil service. The classical liberal-model view of the service treated it as essentially passive and subordinate, carrying out the will of elected rulers. True, even the foundation document, the Northcote-Trevelyan report of 1853, thought that senior civil servants would be of great influence,[76] and in the 1930s Ramsay Muir realised that they were part of 'the government'. But the policy-making approach could accept Government departments and other public bodies as agents within the process—or processes— whereby policies emerged. The crucial point lay in the wide definition of pressure 'group'. Their roles may have differed for constitutional reasons, but all could be realistically appraised within the same conceptual framework.

Even so, it may be doubted whether the propagandists of corporatism or the analysts of policy-making shifted the popular image of British political arrangements very much. It is true that corporatist theory, like pressure group theory before it, could show that processes of the nature described did occur: there was real evidence to support the revised vision. Moreover, this contrasted with the failures of the NEDC and of Select Committees to make more than marginal contributions to effective Government policy. But in terms of the perceptions of informed observers—politicians, journalists, non-specialist academics—the renowned institutions of party, Parliament and Government still loomed very large indeed. As Richard Rose put it, in 1983, it was 'still the era of party government.'[77]

Party government indeed, but was it *two* party government? Or if it was, should this duality be retained? In the 1970s this central feature of the system began to be questioned. One form of attack cast doubt on the historical persistence of the duality. A re-reading of developments since the mid-nineteenth century noted that there were rarely *only* two parties—splinters in the form of the Liberal Unionists, the Lib-Lab MPs, and later the Labour Party itself soon appeared. The Irish party was an important factor until the end of the First World War. Between the wars there was a three-party system until the 1931 election. Coalition was also more common than realised, it was argued.[78]

What was not much in dispute was that the post-1945 period constituted the heyday of two-party competition. The crisis of the 1970s did not decisively end it, but it shook confidence in it. For one thing other parties—nationalist and centre parties—became important. But there was also criticism of the two-party principle itself.

Much of the criticism was brought together in *Adversary Politics*[79] (1975) edited and partly written by S. E. Finer. The thesis was that the two parties were necessarily 'adversarial'—they were combat organisations permanently pitted against each other. The electoral system gave them every chance of alternating in power. Instead of competing for a centre ground, and pursuing the tactics of compromise, the parties had found that they could still win majorities in the Commons by following ideological notions. So there was no consistent State policy—changes swung one way and then another. Legislation by one Government was repealed by the next. In these conditions, it was natural for business, trade unions, and other interests to bide their time and wait for the political wind to change.

The proposition of this school of thought was that more consistent, coherent and sustainable national policies would be achieved if the adversary system was changed. A three-party or multi-party system would mean permanent coalition government. The main means to this end was the introduction of proportional representation in elections. No party would get an outright majority, and so compromise would be necessary in all Governments. In time activists would realise that no absolute victory was possible, and their own tactics and expectations would be adjusted accordingly. National policies would follow a consensual line.

There was a good deal that was speculative about this scheme. To some extent the Liberal-SDP Alliance in the 1980s followed this strategy. However, the important thing for this book lies in the attempts to change the image of what already existed. The denial of two-party hegemony as historical truth was one revision. The picture of widely fluctuating policies, polarised ideologies and the failure to seek a middle ground was another, perhaps the most vivid, alteration in the traditional picture of British civic culture. There were many critics, of course, of both the analysis and the remedies. In any case, the vision did not progress, at any rate for a time. The instability of the 1970s was followed by three majority Conservative governments, which had other ideas for dealing with the crisis.

If a system of proportional representation in elections was securely established, then many other things might change—the practices of Government and Parliament would have to follow a new political logic. Other critics emphasised the weaknesses of contemporary arrangements in face of crisis—new constitutional ideas, for instance, were presented by Nevil Johnson, Lord Hailsham and Owen Hood Phillips.[80] They did not come to anything at the time, but criticism of this nature served to emphasise the insecure nature of the 'flexible' British constitution. So much depended on convention and common understanding: if these were no longer reliable, could the system be stabilised by a new constitution, a system of administrative law, an entrenched bill of rights? Hence there was, close to mainstream opinion, something of a return to 'constitutional' thinking. The rules might be important after all.

Another illustrative change lay in the campaigns for open government and in that for reform or abolition of quasi-governmental bodies, the so-called 'quangos'. The perception of British governmental practice as a highly secretive affair grew apace in the 1970s, and the advocacy of 'freedom of information' legislation became a popular cause. But the practices were not new. The change marked a loss of trust in what went on in ruling circles, both political and bureaucratic.[81]

The 'great quango hunt' was an episode of the early 1980s. It was suddenly alleged that the numerous autonomous and semi-independent bodies—tribunals, advisory committees, councils, and administrative organisations—were anomalous, unaccountable and expensive: and their numbers ought to be reduced.[82] In fact though many advisory committees were abolished or merged, the Government also set up new bodies, particularly in its reform of local government. The significant feature of the controversy, for this study, lay in the fact that it was possible to present the phenomenon as some sort of revelation—as a surprise, indeed 'news'. Awareness was at a low ebb. People did not realise, in this respect at least, how Britain was governed.

COLLECTIVIST DEPARTURE?

In sum, then, what effect did the crisis of the 1970s have for this image of the political system? If the purpose was to examine the facts, then even by the mid-1980s and after two Conservative governments, collectivism had not departed very far. Big government had been reduced a little, public expenditure had been restrained, but big organisations and political parties were still there.

But it is not the purpose here to look at the facts. The mission is to look at images, at what people thought was happening. There was certainly a growing disposition to look beyond these old outlines, to think in terms that did not accept 'collectivist arrival' as the summation of affairs. Some of these other outlooks will be described in later chapters. Two contributions, however, need mention here.

In the late 1970s the old master S. H. Beer returned to the scene he had so vividly described in the 1950s, and found it in disarray. In *Britain Against Itself*[83] (1982) he presented his new version. The key to the trouble lay in 'pluralistic stagnation'. The system of government by party, under pressures from group interests, still remained. But it no longer worked benignly. The interests inside and outside the parties joined in a competitive scramble for benefits, for pay, for subsidies, and for political favours; and the organs of wider concern—the parties, the Government itself—were unable to contain these demands. Or, at least if they did so they lost popular support. The result was a log jam. Radical departures could not take place, for those who supported them in general did not support them in particular circumstances.

The opposition to action came from trade unions, from the City of London, from business, from other groups, and was not, of course, united; but it was usually strong enough to prevent policies from being properly effective. The processes of British policy-making, dependent on consultation and with insecure Governments, did not allow a general will to mobilise support to overcome sectional demands. People might agree that pay, benefits and subsidies should be restrained or controlled—provided other groups had their pay, benefits and subsidies controlled too. But in the absence of certainty about what might happen to others, sectional self-interest always broke through.

Beer goes on to note the growing social convergence: the two great parties found that the class basis of their support was being eroded. Moreover, deference—so long a mainstay of the British system, as writers from Bagehot onwards had affirmed—collapsed in the 1960s and 70s. It was a main factor in a wider decline of their civic culture, something on which the British had been congratulated in the 1950s. A technocratic attack had been frustrated by populist values, which extolled the virtues and possibilities of liberation, and of universal democratic participation. This spread well beyond orthodox political arenas. Many strikes and other rallies, demonstrations, and like actions were valued as rewarding forms of activity in themselves, whatever their practicalities. These actions in turn generated distrust, for many reacted against them.

The other concluding example in this section comes from Anthony King, a Canadian professor of politics at the University of Essex. In 1976, at the height of the crisis he wrote on 'Why is Britain harder to govern?' and advanced a theory of 'overload'.[84] This was not merely an economic or administrative matter—'when government becomes too big, politics becomes big too.'[85] What was overloaded, in King's view, was Government responsibilities—or in other words what the public expected of government. It was not merely a matter of industries being in public ownership—

> That is beside the point, which is that there is now hardly anything in which Government can avoid taking an interest. The distinction between 'private' and 'public' has . . . become hopelessly blurred.[86]

This was caused by public expectations—that the Government would do something to correct any manifest evil, or to remove any weakness in national performance or prestige. But Governments could no longer cope—the 'reach of British Government exceeds its grasp.'[87] The reasons for this state of affairs were partly economic, but more fundamentally lay in the rise in complexity—in the number of 'dependency relations' in government and in society. When something went wrong, it threw a long succession of other things out too. When Governments tried to change or reform something, then an unforeseeable number of side effects brought another range of problems, all demanding further action in turn. Perhaps, as remedies, the duties of Government might be reduced; perhaps people might be persuaded to expect less. But nevertheless, King concluded in 1976 'It is hard not to be a little pessimistic about the future.'[88]

These views illustrate the measure of disillusion with the theories and remedies that had been associated with the arrival of collectivism. Nevertheless, they were views particularly associated with the decade of crisis. Visions change, even the visions of despair.

5   Other Themes, and Discords

In some sense, the substance of political events must be what it is and the truth about them unique. Disputes between historians about what actually happened may possibly be settled by reference to facts—to records. But all history is selective, and some judgments of what is significant and what is not must always be made. The same is true in political studies. The previous section has described what was a dominant view of the British system, of what many people saw and thought was happening. But with a different viewpoint the occurrences themselves may take on a different form. This section discusses the operation of British politics looked at in other ways. What seemed to be happening, if different spectacles were worn?

CONSERVATIVE SCEPTICISM

Though the general term for this theme is 'conservative scepticism', it was not the property of the Conservative party, even if many of those who contributed to it found themselves voting for that party. The defining characteristic lies rather in the scepticism, and particularly in this context scepticism about the growth of government. The scepticism was sometimes thoroughgoing, and included scepticism about the value of democratic pressures, along with a general refusal to get excited abut radical new ideas. Not that all developments were bad; indeed they might be very necessary, certainly as alternatives in difficult situations. On the whole this school takes the view that human folly is fairly constant, and that the task of government is to minimise its consequences.

In the period in question, one political philosopher, Michael Oakeshott, had great influence for these sceptics. Not that all writers to be mentioned are Oakeshottians: no such sharp definition would be justified. The influence relevant to this study is diffuse in nature, and in any case is not the ultimate philosophical impact. It may well be that most interpretations of Oakeshott's writings, at any level, are misinterpretations. However the fame of some of his phrases has spread, and these have had consequences, intended or otherwise, for political attitudes. For instance:

> In political activity then, men sail a boundless and bottomless sea; there is neither harbour for shelter nor floor for anchorage, neither starting-place nor appointed destination. The enterprise is to keep afloat on an even keel; the sea is both friend and enemy; and the seamanship consists in using the resources of a traditional manner of behaviour in order to make a friend of every hostile occasion.[1]

This non-directional movement is another hallmark of conservative scepticism: polities are not going anywhere.

If the arrival of collectivism is not to be welcomed, how might it be viewed? Phlegmatic resignation might be appropriate—after all, not dissimilar things were happening in other countries. One possibility was to see collectivist arrival as another turn in a cyclical rotation. Another possibility was to see it as dependent on illusion, primarily economic. Nevil Johnson wrote, in 1975, about the post-war era:

> The country endowed with material and human resources vastly less than those possessed by the two world powers, had impoverished itself in an effort which also, as one can see in retrospect, appears to have drained it of much of its creative energy. In sober practical terms the British people ought in 1945 to have been confronted with the reality of their economic situation . . . Instead, as if in a great spasm of emotional relief, Britain began to move into the realm of illusion.[2]

Could this illusion have been avoided? An explicit choice, with political consequences, would have been necessary.

> Part of the problem was that the 1945 Labour Government *could* not make such an explicit choice, whilst its Conservative successors were too lazy and foolish even to see the need for it.[3]

The myth that disguised reality took the form of the substitution of governmental economic management for individual economic motivation. This view overlapped with that of the next theme, that of the market liberals. The quotations are from a book *In Search of the Constitution* in which a political remedy—a new constitutional settlement— was advocated.[4] Advocating remedies of any sort, let alone those involving institutional change, was not considered a proper academic pursuit by many writers of this school. However, there were in Johnson's book some characteristics which do fit the image—the distrust of over-ambitious ideals, the duty of wise leadership, the dangers of indulgence.

It is certainly fair to attribute to this outlook longer historical perspectives than those usually found elsewhere. The collectivist mood of the times might inspire no confidence, but for these conservatives there had been many other episodes in the past where overoptimistic creeds had taken public fancy. Such passions were dangerous if they lasted too long, or went to extremes, or destroyed valuable stabilising social institutions. Nevertheless things could be worse—revolution, tyranny, disorder were also possible in the future as in the past. So while scepticism about current trends, especially about the capabilities of government to promote human welfare, was always to the fore in this school, an awareness of the needs of statesmen to satisfy vulgar expectations was also present. The ship had to be kept afloat.

With this preference for the historical view went a dislike of models of the system: indeed the conception of a 'system' was probably a misconception in itself. Any attempt to provide a mechanistic account of the British polity was doomed to failure—the working of particular institutions might be described, of course, but no collection of such accounts could add up to a general understanding. Any appreciation of the nature of arrangements that went beyond such descriptions or legalities would have to accept the organic relationships of people and institutions, past and present.

It is tempting to see this mood as a sort of revival of the philosophy of Edmund Burke. There are certainly Burkean reflections from time to time, but in fact the patron philosophers of this tendency are Hobbes and Hegel, and it stems from the English interpreters and successors of Hegel in the nineteenth century and earlier twentieth century. Its political mentor was Lord Salisbury. The mention of John Stuart Mill causes apoplexy. Nevertheless, as regards writers on British politics, the recommendation was to look to the practical men of affairs themselves, and to discount the prescriptions of academic scholars, who were exceeding their proper competence.

Nevertheless, the outlook may be further illustrated by attitudes to the practical politics of the period. Nobody holds all these views (any more than they do in other sections) but they exhibit the spirit of things.

First there was a certain nostalgia for the days of imperial power. Perhaps the economic and political practicalities which brought about the end of empire could be accepted. But there was no reason to accept that this was for the good. Worst of all was any sense of guilt, that imperial rule or colonial government were things of shame. For this school of thought such views amounted to sentimentalism and hypocrisy. The spread of colonial possessions had been another chapter of history (indeed like collectivism itself) that could be attributed to historical circumstances. It brought benefits of relatively peaceful rule, unity and order to many areas, and its departure did not often bring practical benefits. To suggest that 'alien rule' or imperialism was wrong in itself was moral cant.

In his essay 'A New International Disorder' (1980) Elie Kedourie wrote:

> 'Decolonisation' suddenly became the settled policy of the British, the French and the Belgians, a policy precipitately and thoroughly applied whatever the costs and consequences. The policy was, by and large, the outcome of a unilateral decision taken by the metropolitan authorities, rather than a response

to some overwhelming or irresistible pressure exerted by the African populations. The decision was based on a judgment about the worth to the metropolitan countries of administering these colonies . . . There was in these judgments a large element of defeatism, complacency, cynicism and sheer illusion.[5]

A second example may be drawn from the attempts of the state to promote social welfare. Since care of the poor was an old function of the state, and insurance a growing aspect of social life, then these might possibly form an acceptable development, at least on a limited scale. Folly lay in over-ambition, and corruption in the practice of appealing for votes by promising greater benefits. Certainly any attempt to use such a system to change the social order was scouted.

Thirdly it may be asked what attitudes there were towards the political or governmental reforms so popular with the collectivist school. Commonly there is a measured sense of constitutional propriety

We need to regain some sense of institutions as the means by which authority is created and made effective, and to escape from a world in which institutions have been degraded to 'machinery of government', 'management and organisation' or simply 'dignified scenery', lending respectability to the demands of those with the loudest voices.[6]

The poet and civil servant C. H. Sisson, wrote in 1959 on *The Spirit of British Administration*. He held an extremely high view of the possibilities of administrative detachment:

There is no need for the administrator to be a man of ideas. His distinguishing quality should be a certain freedom from ideas. The idealisms and the most vicious appetites of the populace are equal before him. He should be prepared to bow before any wisdom whose mouth is loud enough.[7]

Could this be? On the whole other writers while discouraging administrative ambitions and certainly disbelieving claims for either scientific or creative administration, expected more than mechanical competence from higher civil servants. Wisdom bred of experience might well emanate from this quarter.

However, the urge to constitutional propriety was accompanied by a belief that authority, and hence government, ought to be respected; and it should not be afraid to rule. The reliance on pressure groups which had become accepted was therefore regarded with some suspicion, for it might lead to a habit of dependence on them, and hence an abdication of responsibility. Twentieth century democracy required political parties and pressure groups, and so they were not to be ignored. But one of the disadvantages of democracy was that it encouraged political enthusiasts, and though these people were not without their due role in society, they were not well suited to the activity of governing. Wise rulers kept their distance. Thus the picture of British political arrangements seen through this particular window was still primarily composed of traditional institutions—Crown, Ministers, Parliament, the Courts, the armed services, and local authorities, (buttressed by some private but established bodies) and the vigorous organisations and groups elevated to such importance in other eyes were for all their power, somehow secondary and probably temporary.

Indeed there was a certain uneasiness, even ambivalence to be noted in these matters. There was, of course, an inclination to respect constitutional traditions, formulated by A. V. Dicey or similar authorities. But this gave scope to the opportunities provided by parliamentary sovereignty and an unwritten constitution. Was the traditional way of the constitution really rigid enough? Flexibility might be a safeguard against revolution, under stress, but was it not being exploited by hyperactive legislators? Law was certainly preferred to legislation but it was never clear how much practical guidance could be expected from such a principle.

Similar variations might be noted elsewhere. In general there was respect for central authority and what amounted to a preference for what Birch called the 'Whitehall' view of the system, to protect national unity; but on the other hand there were those who saw in decentralisation, to localities or even to the countries of the United Kingdom, some hope of political security—and even more important, more chance of resisting false ideologies.

The attitude to central control sometimes proceeded along high politics/low politics lines. The centre should have complete control of certain matters—foreign policy, defence, national finance, macroeconomic policy—free from local or regional pressures. Other 'lower' matters, however, should be left to other bodies provided they did not challenge the central power.[8]

For those with outlooks appropriate to this section, there can be little question that high politics has the most crucial social task, in its management of low politics. Indeed such business was the main activity of the state. There will be change, and often this can be regarded as progress, an improvement in standards. It was unlikely to be moral or political in character, nor was it the function of politics to promote changes. Society in Britain as elsewhere was difficult to govern at any time: the prospects of 'steering' it through revolution or other convulsions were non-existent. So drastic change was to be avoided. Statesmen should try not to fight great battles.

The crisis of the 1970s in British politics fitted well into the expectations of this outlook, in that it demonstrated the futility of liberal and socialist notions. The bubble of optimistic illusion had burst, and for a time rational pessimism could influence authority. The economic remedies favoured were similar to those of the market liberals—the restoration of a sound currency, reduction of public expenditure, and 'an end to promises'.[9] With this school however, there was a moral and political edge to the prescription. The free economy was the proper way to run the economy as such. The state, however, was not to be understood on these lines. Authority, morality, tradition, necessity, order were the watchwords in this context. Nor could there be a mere anarchy of opinions: unity and cohesion could not be achieved with total openness. 'Every society must be closed to some degree'[10] wrote Shirley Letwin. In that sense, then, shorn of its illusions, consensus might be no bad thing after all.

One vision of British politics, conformable in mood at any rate to this school, was provided by the work of W. H. Greenleaf, Professor of Politics at the University College of Swansea. There was, first, an article entitled 'The Character of

Modern British Politics'. That character 'is indicated by the antithesis of extreme features within which confines its behaviour falls. These delimit its typical style or way of acting.'[11] There were two opposing tendencies, or 'a rhythm between two opposing states'. The concepts were not mere abstractions—they were 'immanent in the concrete historical reality of British politics itself.'[12]

The two concepts were libertarianism and collectivism. Libertarianism had four aspects: individual freedom; a consequential limitation on government; a diffusion of decision and authority; and the rule of law. It was not uniform and covered a range of emphases—indeed it could not display a nuclear character.

The dominant feature of collectivism was concern for the public good. Community claims and social justice took precedence over any individual demand. Action on the part of public authority was required to sustain these principles, though of course there were great differences in degree or manner of what was proposed or brought about. On the whole this concept had had most influence in Britain over the last fifty years.

There were obvious resemblances between this dichotomy and the distinction made by Beer between the Liberal theory and that of the collectivist age. The main source however was A. V. Dicey's *Law and Public Opinion*[13] of 1905. All these writers accepted the obvious ascendancy of collectivism. Nevertheless, for Greenleaf the doctrines were not simply partisan—indeed, they were hardly partisan at all in the long run. There were Conservative, Liberal and Socialist versions of both tendencies, in ascendancy in the parties at different times.

Many writers of this outlook have extolled the virtues of the British tradition, and of its value in guiding political action. In four great volumes, which began publication in 1983, W. H. Greenleaf took the trouble to understand and explain this tradition and to expand it at length. In the second volume, *The Ideological Heritage*,[14] he again insists

> Instead of nuclear designation . . . it is necessary to establish the character of an ideology by, first, admitting the inevitability of diversity and change and then, secondly, by delimiting this variety

through observation of the extreme and opposition manifestations . . .[15]

The volume consists of extended analysis of three ideologies, Liberalism, Conservatism and Socialism on these lines. 'Each doctrine thus nurtures two conflicting or contrasting modes of thought; and the history of modern ideological opinion is generally an 'oscillation between these extremes.'[16] The facts of twentieth-century changes were there to be seen: but the collectivist arrival was not an historical climax or culmination. It was a phase in an oscillation, an emphasis in a tension of rival ideas that has long existed—and though the future could not be predicted, the oscillations might well go on. There was no manifest destiny in this outlook. There was oscillation, and any acceptance of collectivist arrival might merely precede collectivist departure—or at any rate, the emphases might change, within a continuing tension.

It would be wrong to suggest that the urbane, eclectic and elegant volumes of Greenleaf were themselves ideological, except in the sense that some preconceptions must always colour an author's judgment. They were not works of advocacy. The point of mentioning them here, rather than elsewhere, is to draw attention to the emphasis on the tradition of ideas as the vital clue to understanding a polity. There was noticeably less emphasis on authority than some other authors in this section were inclined to give. Nevertheless, respect for tradition, in intellectual terms; a long historical perspective; a preference for order; and a mistrust of romantic idealism were all there. Relaxed and tolerant as they were, nevertheless their rightful home was among the traditionalists.

MARKET LIBERATION

A second school of thought which found little to admire in the arrival of collectivism, was that of 'market liberation'. Belief in the importance of free enterprise in business and of market freedoms in trading and in labour matters has been a main principle of liberal thought at least since Adam Smith's book on the *Wealth of Nations* in 1776. However, Smith was a Whig and a moderate. The school of thought relevant to this study is radical and sometimes uncompromising. Though its policy attitudes are similar to those writers mentioned in the previous section, its outlook is neither conservative nor sceptical.

The distinguishing feature which marked it out was that it saw the whole tendency to governmental action, since the mid-nineteenth century, as a mistake. It was not only a British mistake, but the errors and the effects were particularly bad in Britain. There was not much acknowledgment of prudent political flexibility, or of an oscillation of ideas: the trend was always wrong. Pragmatism may have had its place in other political matters but not in this. Most of the philosophising behind these attitudes stems from economic reasoning, but not all, as the examples of Herbert Spencer in the nineteenth century and Robert Nozick in the 1970s showed.

In fact the outlook had its guiding philosopher. F. A. Hayek was born and educated in Austria but was at the London School of Economics from 1931 to 1950 and directly acquainted with British affairs from that time. Since then he lived in the United States and in Germany. His most popular book was *The Road to Serfdom*[17] first published in 1944, and reissued in 1976. It was dedicated to the 'socialists of all parties' and begins with a chapter 'The Abandoned Road'. This road was not a recent one:

> We are rapidly abandoning not merely the views of Cobden and Bright, of Adam Smith and Hume . . . but one of the salient characteristics of Western civilisation as it has grown from the foundations laid by Christianity and the Greeks and Romans.[18] [or again:], The change amounts to a complete reversal of the trend . . . an entire abandonment of the individualist tradition which has created Western civilisation.[19]

The essential change was the abandonment of the belief in making the best use of spontaneous forces in a free society, and its replacement by a belief in collective and conscious direction of all social forces to deliberately chosen goals. This redirection he attributed to German intellectual influences.[20]

Hayek also wrote an essay 'Why I am not a conservative' which was reprinted in *The Constitution of Liberty*[21] (1960). It emphasises several distinguishing features of this outlook. The decisive reason for not supporting conservatism was 'that by its very nature it cannot offer an alternative to the direction in which we are moving.' Liberalism 'wants to go elsewhere, not stand still.'[22] Moreover, conservatism fears uncontrolled social forces and is too complacent about established authority. It is hostile to internationalism.

Crucially, perhaps, for many of this school traditional conservatism offered too little hope. It was too pessimistic about the future. In contrast to the conservative sceptics, moreover, most of these writers were anti-Hegelian.

For the sake of clarity something needs to be said about monetarism. Most writers of this tendency endorsed monetarist principles, in that they believed that inflation could be reduced by firm control of the money supply. The special influence of this doctrine was due to empirical research by Milton Friedman,[23] a professor of economics at the University of Chicago. Hayek favoured the policy strongly, though he was not an empiricist in methodology. There was indeed a political reason why the doctrine attracted this school—it offered less scope for Government discretion.

No doubt it would have been better to take monetary matters entirely out of the hands of Government. Short of that, a fixed rule for the supply of money seemed the best available option. In spite of its popularity at this time, however, monetarism was a relatively technical economic device. The wider principles at stake were those of the free market, and it is on these that political exposition must focus.

What image of the British political system was engendered by this outlook? In general, it was seen as a system particularly vulnerable to pressure. Its institutions and its flexible constitution provided no barrier to the encroachment of special interests. Since 1867 politicians have been disastrously subject to the temptation to promise State benefits in exchange for votes. The rule of law, which was once the key to British constitutionality had been ruinously misinterpreted and eroded.

For most of the period it is easier to say what was opposed than what was supported.

In the particular circumstances, the development of pressure groups was seen as especially retrograde. They were regarded not as constructive intermediary bodies in a complex polity, but as the means of biassing what should be impartial decisions. Worse, they encouraged Governments to do things. Often these actions seemed to be morally or socially urgent; but they were in any case likely to be in the interest of a section of the community rather than the whole. State action was in any case undesirable, since it depended on compulsory taxation and was inherently bureaucratic and inefficient. Pressure groups turned people's attention away from alternative action through private enterprise or voluntary means.

Indeed, it was a prime characteristic of this school that it concentrated attention on the relations between politics (interpreted to mean government) and the economy. In any conflict the needs and values of the economy were paramount.

The practical applications of this philosophy to the British system of government, largely of course in the 1980s, showed up some of its characteristics and some of its problems. Like other outlooks, it could not secure individual dominance— even its apparent adherents were also influenced by conservative scepticism, radical modernisation and mainstream ideas. There was nothing surprising or unusual about this. But it obviously precluded an application of the uncompromising approach that its philosophy required. In this matter it reflected—from an opposing point of view—the attitudes of the left, where the political entanglements of the actual world cause embarrassment.

This mirror-image was apparent in another way. Being progressive and future-oriented, rather than conservative and stabilising, the enthusiasts in the Conservative government proceeded with a programme of privatisation in industry. Like the previous move to nationalisation, this policy was gradualistic and industry by industry; it was pragmatic in that the sequence and particularities were opportunistic and practical; and its ultimate objective was dogmatic and ideological. Privatisation like nationalisation could be, for its visionaries, total and complete.

More light on this general view of the system was thrown by the writings of Samuel Brittan, a senior journalist on *The Financial Times*. On the whole he was a moderate adherent of this viewpoint, but an influential one in the 1970s. He is particularly relevant to this book for his concern with the political system.

One book of his, *Capitalism and the Permissive Society*[24] (1973) pointed out the libertarian foundations of these two concepts. Brittan supported both, as he later confirmed,[25] and refused to join the Conservative Party when he found that it did not support the latter. The collection of essays in *The Economic Consequences of Democracy*[26] (1977) contained the main theses. Brittan argued that 'Two endemic threats to liberal representative democracy are: (a) the generation of excessive expectations; and (b) the disruptive effects of the pursuit of group self-interest in the market place.'[27] His basic theory of democracy was that of Schumpeter, a competition for power between competing teams, not a means of popular participation nor a means for putting into practice the people's will.[28] The threats he mentioned had become more serious, because there was no longer a widely shared belief in the legitimacy of the existing order; but neither was there any commonly-held conception of a feasible alternative order. Indeed, he goes on to attack the validity of any sort of concept of social justice, which might have served as the basis of such an alternative.[29]

The threats were of course, brought about by the operation of democratic processes themselves. Since budget constraints were not apparent to voters as such, they tended to vote for more benefits, more well-being, and for promises of economic growth. Politicians in their own interests encouraged these expectations: 'Democracy, viewed as a process of political competition, itself imparts a systematic bias to expectations and compounds the other influences at work.'[30] Self-interested groups, with possibly damaging effects, could exist in all sorts of political systems. However, the 'liberal' aspects of democracy made it difficult to tackle them properly. These tensions were particularly acute in the United Kingdom.

Two comparisons may be made. In the first place this analysis was greatly reminiscent of the criticism of democracy in Victorian controversies. Brittan referred to Bagehot's fears and quoted the historian J. A. Froude. He might have said more. The political literature of the period on this topic was much richer than he acknowledged. For about a hundred years the critics were believed to be wrong—deference survived, the Conservative Party flourished, governments coped with the changing expectations and concerns of voters, and other countries were urged to adopt similar free electoral systems. In comparative analyses of political cultures, Britain was always listed as a 'stable democracy'. Brittan's rediscovery of the problems was strangely delayed.

The other comparison is with the mainstream model of S. H. Beer. Here too, there was competition between parties, but it was believed to moderate party policies, or at any rate to make sure that they appealed to non-ideological members of the electorate. In this model too, pressure groups act as a supplementary democratic addition to the main system. Brittan's interpretation substitutes a malign account of what had been treated as a benign process. Instead of debate and discussion, he saw a political and economic share-out: the parties competed for power in order to benefit their clients, and interest groups (especially trade unions) used their strength in the economy to increase their well-being at the expense of weaker sections.

Unlike Hayek and other theorists, Brittan did not look for purity:

> Casual historical observation suggests that democracies can carry on almost indefinitely subsidizing prestige high-technology activities such as aerospace, protecting inefficient farmers, imposing tariffs and quotas, encouraging union restrictive practices, rigging interest rates for favoured groups, 'supporting' key prices . . . preserving monopoly rights for state industries and carrying out hosts of similar welfare-reducing actions, without producing catastrophic results or even preventing a considerable advance in living standards.[31]

This might not seem too bad. However, these negative features cannot accumulate for ever, and sooner or later circumstances will bring crisis.

Brittan's activities brought him a good deal nearer to political practice than some more profound thinkers. There was no doubt that on the whole democracy was regarded with suspicion by the high philosophers of this school. The prime value was liberty, and indeed liberty of action before liberty of expression. But mundane politicians in countries like Britain felt it necessary to support democratic values too, and so the great vision was clouded and confused.

It was sometimes difficult to see how redemption could occur, in a democratic society, given the inherent nature of the forces which were diagnosed. However, since this was an optimistic rather than a pessimistic creed, remedies were proposed. The classic recourse of this school was to limit the effects of democratic politics, the politics of votes and the politics of pressure, by constitutional restriction—by establishing rules which would prevent at least the worst effects of the system.

In *The Disease of Government*[32] (1978) H. S. Ferns, Professor of Political Science at the University of Birmingham, proposed constitutional devices to end 'auction politics'. This disease was worse in Britain than elsewhere owing to the unlimited sovereignty of the 'Crown in Parliament'. To curtail the effects of the political auction two constitutional rights should be created: (i) an absolute right for citizens to hold assets in any currency of any country; and (ii) the Goverment's taxation rights should be confined to income taxes, and the size of the public debt should be limited. These devices were intended to prevent any Government from attempting to 'manage' the economy.[33]

Other reformers were less specific in their economic orientation. Lord Hailsham, though hitherto not regarded as a market liberator, in 1978 criticised the constitutional system as one of 'elective dictatorship'[34] and proposed reforms, principally a written constitution.

> But the real necessity is to limit the unlimited powers of the legislature, partly by establishing a new system of checks and balances, partly by devolution, and partly by restricting the power of Parliament to infringe the rights of minorities and individuals.[35]

The object of the new constitution 'should be to institutionalize the theory of limited government'. This might fit with market liberation views, but Lord Hailsham also stated: 'In recent years change has been too rapid, that is too rapid for the public mind to digest, or the need for continuity to accept.'[36] This sounds properly Conservative. In 1979 Lord Hailsham joined Mrs. Thatcher's government, which did not attempt a written constitution, but did proceed with rapid discontinuous change.

Beyond these issues the general implications were more difficult to discern. Since it was a form of individualism, it was formally opposed to nationalism—though rarely so vigorously as it opposed socialism. Free trade in goods and services, and free flow of capital, were strongly recommended; advocacy of free immigration was less in evidence. Most people in sympathy with this outlook inherited anti-imperialist views from classical liberals: however, they also disliked new nationalisms since these encouraged restriction and distortion in economic systems, and claimed 'aid' for economic purposes. As in democratic politics, the key to foreign affairs lay in approval of régimes which had open economic systems: other qualities were secondary.

This tendency to subordinate other matters to the overriding economic imperative could also be seen in matters of governmental structure and administration. Reduction in public expenditure was mainly pursued by reduction of the scope and variety of governmental activities. But public expenditure was also restrained by a tight fiscal control of whatever was undertaken. In the abstract a liberal outlook might have led to ideas of decentralisation and autonomy, for local and other institutions. In practice with market liberators, the urge to financial control and to limit activity was decisive, and they therefore supported strong central control and managerial direction in administrative matters. There must be some question, however, whether this trend was really a part of the creed of market liberation, but was (like the hostility to permissiveness) rather the practical consequence, in Britain, of the fact that these economic doctrines were put into effect by a Government whose other source of inspiration was traditional Toryism.

There was in association with this theory of market liberation some political speculation about 'ungovernability'. The links lay in the problem of govermental capability and public expectations. The theory of Anthony King about 'overload', brought about by popular assumptions has been mentioned in the previous chapter. The root of governmental incapacity according to F. A. Hayek lay in the impossibility of assembling in any central institution sufficient information to make the multitude of economic decisions necessary in society. For the analysts of 'ungovernability' the issue was less dramatic—their question was about the viability of existing governments.

This turned on whether economic growth (difficult to keep up in Britain) could sustain a tax-base sufficient to cope with inbuilt assumptions in the public services. This is, however, an empirical question, and though some writers linked the problems in terms of dramatic fiscal crises[37] and other forms of breakdown, the connections were on the whole opportunist. For true market liberators, Government activity and intervention were always bad and always inefficient. Crises merely showed that things were even worse than usual.

The three questions asked about other themes can be posed again. Market liberation had little to say about any relation between high politics and low: a state elite might have emerged, but it was undesirable and should be diminished, by the free play of market forces and the restriction of state activities giving such an elite little scope. As explained, the historical image of this view was that of a good world gone wrong, and so a sharp reverse turn was advocated by some, including Hayek. The rejection of much previous political development was a marked feature of this outlook. Progress was conceived as an inextricably-linked rise in material well-being and individual liberty, measured by absence of restrictions. Such matters as national power and prestige were irrelevant (except as means of protecting liberty) and social justice was a bogus concept.

CLASS CONFLICT

Very different thoughts were to be found among those whose image of the British system centred on class conflict—a conflict sometimes partly submerged and sometimes breaking out into open struggle. For these thinkers it was always this conflict that was the key to interpretation. Other features might apparently dominate the scene, but they could only be understood in a fundamental sense, by class analysis.

The body of this work was of course, in some form Marxist. However, not only were there many Marxist ideas but some so far strayed from orthodoxy that they did not fit that description in any strict sense.

(a) In the post-war revival of Marxist analysis of British politics the pioneering works were those of Ralph Miliband. He was a student of Harold Laski at the London School of Economics, and later a lecturer there; and then professor of politics at the University of Leeds. In *Parliamentary Socialism*[38] (1961) he recounted the history of the Labour Party in terms of its commitment to parliamentarianism and lack of commitment to real socialist purposes. It was a refutation of his mentor Laski's view that there was a fundamental gulf between Labour and the other parties.

In *The State in Capitalist Society*[39] (1969) he analysed the way in which the state was controlled by capitalist interests. Thus (in contrast to both the collectivist arrival school and the market liberators) state industries and state-run services were not to be regarded as socialist or even socialist-inclined institutions. The great changes in government activity since 1867—including those after 1945—were essentially manoeuvres whereby capitalism retained control in different ways. True, some concessions were made in order to appease the most urgent discontents. But state services were controlled by people from the capitalist class, and were run in its interests. State interference, he argued,

> is not in fundamental opposition to the interests of property: it is indeed part of that 'ransom' of which Joseph Chamberlain spoke in 1885 and which he said would have to be paid precisely for the purpose of *maintaining* the rights of property in general.[40]

This argument transformed the position of the state and the state sector for the left in British politics. Unlike the old Fabian tradition, which had regarded state activities as part of a gradual transition to socialism, for this outlook they were part of capitalism and therefore a legitimate target of hostility.

This analysis also provided the essential clue to the events of the 1970s. The ransom being demanded by the working people was becoming too great, thus forcing up the rate of inflation. In order to avoid paying this price any longer, the ruling class shifted its policy to one of curbing working class power—by monetarist finance, by unemployment and legal and police repression of trade unions. The motive for these changes, in this vision, was not primarily economic reform but retaining political power.

For the purpose of this book Miliband's *Capitalist Democracy in Britain*[41] (1982) provides the most convenient guide to his ideas

> The different elements of the British political system constitute a system of containment; and . . . that the nature and function of these different elements are best understood if they are seen as part of such a system.[42] [Furthermore,] . . . it is a crucial concern of those who run the state and other institutions of power to achieve the containment and reduction of popular pressure.[43]

He argued that Parliament was the central institution of the system. The extension of the franchise from 1867 had been designed to encourage the rising social forces of labour to participate in the existing system, and so divert them from anti-system activities. Trade unions were contained by giving their leaders roles within the system, and by propaganda counselling moderation. The media filtered, distorted and softened news of radical discontent. The main pressures to which government was subject were those of capital and labour; they were antagonistic, but the state had always wanted capitalistic enterprise to prosper. This was true under Labour governments, who never wanted public enterprise to be the dominant sector. Similar containment prevailed in local government. Miliband did not believe that the State, or its Government had no autonomy at all; but its freedom of action was limited by capitalist power.

There were various possibilities.[44] The system might carry on, but economic decline would aggravate problems, and the major agency of pressure would be the working class, in the form of organised labour and of voters. This might lead to reaction and the development of a 'strong state' and a form of conservative authoritarianism. The possibility of a Labour government, with a majority, carrying out real socialist change was remote, since in spite of activists within their ranks, the leaders of the Labour party were opposed to any such transformation.

Here again, in this analysis, agencies and forces previously discussed appear. The vision was nevertheless in stark contrast. Pressure groups that mattered in the long run would be from the working class: the real issue was social transformation. Contrary to the presumptions in other schools of thought, they had hitherto only very limited and temporary successes. No fundamental changes so far had been allowed.

Like Brittan and Victorian critics, Miliband saw the potentialities of attacks on property and wealth distribution arising from the widening of the franchise. Unlike them, he was in full support of such attacks. For him, the intellectual problem was to explain why they had achieved so little: hence the theory of containment. Similarly, his view of the existence of a ruling class in Britain had much in common with that of conservative sceptics; but they thought it a vital necessity while he wished to end it. The view that he put forward, of some rulers fearful of democratic pressures and of financial depredations, was well substantiated in the literature, though what the fear was about was less clear.

There was obvious contrast for this view compared with others in the assessment of trade union power and success. David Coates of the University of Leeds, argued in *Labour in Power?* (1980) that the experience of the Labour government of 1974–9 showed the weakness of the movement for socialist purposes:[45]

> The hope of Labour radicals to use Parliament as an alternative to the social and industrial power of the working class could not be more misplaced.[46] [In consequence], What the Left has to build is a renewed *socialist culture*, by fighting on a broad front against the manifestations of capitalist cultural hegemony within the labour movement itself.[47]

It was, therefore, fundamental to this view that there was a deep cleavage in British politics. It did not lie, however, *between* the great parties. Indeed these writers might have accepted Robert McKenzie's argument that at this level there was no deep gulf. The chasm lay *within* the Labour movement. It was the split between 'the Left' and the rest that mattered. For only this line distinguished those who wanted class-conscious socialist change from those who opposed or doubted it.

In contrast to the attitude of the market liberators, the class conflict school saw too many barriers in the system for popular power to be effective. True, the barriers were not the constitutional limitations that some suggested. They were rather the systematic biasses that wealth, privileged education, social prejudice and media influence brought about. Some Marxists, such as Tom Nairn, saw a particular British phenomenon, similar to that of the radical modernisers discussed later:

> Any actual programme of crash 'modernisation' is bound to mean things like this. It implies giving up a lot of the good, comfortable habits everyone depends on, as well as the notorious bad habits holding us back. These comfortable habits include the way we are ruled.[48]

The influence of the City of London and the emphasis given to overseas payments was especially harmful. So the class system, while common in the Marxist view to all capitalist countries, had even worse characteristics in Britain.

The view that the fundamental truth about British politics lay in the existence of a class struggle was held, of course, by all Marxist parties and groups to the left of the Labour Party. A textbook published in 1958 gave a communist version: 'In Britain the greater part of industry, trade, finance and the land is the private property of a small minority of the population.'[49] It went on to document in some detail how this class, and its connections and allies, dominated the many institutions of government, so that there was permanent bias against various minorities, and against the working-class majority.

In general terms all the Trotskyist groups, being committed to Marxism-Leninism, shared this perspective, though often holding sharply conflicting interpretations of the state of the class war at any time, and consequently of appropriate tactics.

The most famous of these was that associated with the publication *Militant* (descended from the Revolutionary Socialist League of 1950s). Unlike other groups it pursued a strategy of 'entrism'—that is, of joining the Labour Party since that was the existing mass organisation, and trying to convert it to more revolutionary ways.[50]

(b) Class conflict is also a feature in pictures of the system less strictly Marxist than the foregoing. Some of these are 'marxisant' in that they use Marxist language without conforming to the principles of the master. Others are developments of the original—neo-Marxist perhaps—and others merely use class analysis in their own way.

In *The Conservative Nation*[51] (1974) Andrew Gamble portrayed the Conservative party's values as essentially national:

> The existence of the Conservative Nation has enormously increased the stability of the British state, and thereby protected the rights and interests of property. Yet the leaders of the Conservative party did not create the Conservative Nation out of nothing. They recognised what already existed.[52]

In *Britain in Decline*[53] he postulated an unfinished revolution. Britain had neither an open mobile society like the United States nor a close nationalistic partnership between government and business as in Germany.[54] In this lay the roots of decline. The capitalist order was threatened by the rise of the Labour movement. This was successfully contained in the 1920s and afterwards; nevertheless 'in spite of the efforts of its leaders'[55] the Labour party never succeeded in ridding itself of its class character—it never completely accepted capitalism ideologically

> The way in which the working class was eventually incorporated preserved property and preserved the existing state; it averted social revolution but it is also put major obstacles in the path of a successful capitalism.[56]

There was consensus on many things, but not on the means for industrial modernisation. So the necessary changes in Britain had been frustrated by the political situation. The capitalist class could not carry them out because of the entrenched power of Labour; but the Labour movement was not able to secure a socialist transformation. Other writers, some of them socialists, also argued that one cause of British decline was the special strength of trade unions, not in general political terms, but in the factories themselves.[57] This long-standing strength made employers avoid technical change if possible, since troublesome negotiations, at least, were necessary. So the vision of British politics put forward is essentially one of a deadlocked system. Hence there is crisis; and though immediate responses to crisis may be reassertions of capitalist power, eventually worsening crises will bring socialist triumph, because that is the way society must go.

A bifurcated image of British politics is presented by John Dearlove and Peter Saunders in a long book *Introduction to British Politics*[58] (1984). They suggest that British political scientists have overstressed democracy, and failed to stress capitalism: '. . . the mere mention of capitalism has been dismissed as a coarse ideological irrelevance.'[59] A smaller Marxist tradition, however, fails to take democracy seriously. Both views have blindspots. In order to remedy this, power in all its aspects must be studied. The outcome is a very complex picture which attempts to incorporate several points of view within the plan of the book.

The resulting analysis was not a Marxist one, nor even a class-conflict one as such. It was only by comparison with non-Marxist writings that it leant that way. They gave emphasis to institutions 'below the democratic froth'.[60] These included the civil service, the nationalised industries, the judiciary, the police, the security services and the military. Their sociological analysis of power in British society led to the conclusion that there was indeed a system of domination: but that no one group totally controlled or consciously manipulated it.[61] Again, though they found that Marxist studies had shown the inadequacies of liberal democratic theories, there was no adequate Marxist explanation of the relationship between the economy and the political system. So they ended as they began—analysis must extend not only beyond the constitutional forms but beyond the political system itself to the power-relations of society. However, no decisive conclusions were to be found, even when class relations were taken into account.

One possible way of restoring class conflict to the centre of the picture of British politics would be to redefine the classes which are involved. This approach would take observers a long way from Marxism, in which the classes are determined by their relations to the means of production. In fact, the voting studies discussed in the previous chapter always ignored these Marxist categories in favour of occupationally-defined classes, as used in market research.

As argued, class analysis in this sense was perfectly acceptable to the mainstream 'collectivist arrival' interpretation. A high degree of class voting brought about that governmental development, and did not threaten to overturn it; and its alleged decline is a matter of some partisan importance, but not destructive of the social order. On the other hand, it is worth noting that the two themes explained so far in this chapter, conservative scepticism and market liberation, do not have much use for class analyses, or class-based explanations of any sort. So even revised definitions of class (so that they are scarcely classes at all) and new theories associated with them find more attention and sympathy among radical spirits. A real class-struggle explanation must give the phenomenon greater emphasis than mere voting; but since it is in social forms that the Left looks for change, so its writers look in this direction. Often, indeed, in post-war Britain they have not found it. The class-struggle theme rarely plays on empirical research.

How did this interpretation answer the three questions? Class conflict visions of British politics had everything to say about the high/low distinction. They had, of course, a specific angle on that distinction. High politics was in part a show (almost Bagehot-style) which—though earnest enough for its participants—was put on to lull the masses into a false sense of self-government. Insofar as it was real, it was about different strategies of retaining class power, for certainly these different strategies might affect segments of the ruling class in different ways. Progress was ultimately both material and spiritual in the sense that human alienation might sometime be ended: but this was not to be measured in current increases in the standard of living. For ultimately a great break would be needed (not necessarily in a short time or involving violence) which would transform class power. In the meantime, for the stricter Marxists, desirable changes were those which increased the morale, solidarity and awareness of the working class. For others, it was more a question of widening democratic influences, so as to break up the hegemony of the closed British ruling elite.

RADICAL MODERNISATION

For some observers, the main characteristic of the British political system was that it was out-of-date.

They did not necessarily differ from mainstream analysts in description of the existing arrangements. As they saw it, however, no adequate process of adaptation or dialectic of change was at work. Whatever had led to British political and economic success in the past was now failing to operate. The opening lines of the Fulton Report on *The Civil Service*[62] gave an illustration of the outlook:

> The Home Civil Service today is still fundamentally the product of the nineteenth century philosophy of the Northcote-Trevelyan Report. The tasks it faces are those of the second half of the twentieth century. This is what we have found; it is what we seek to remedy.[63]

There had been a line of criticism of the efficiency of British society since the nineteenth century. Much of it, then and in the post-war period, was directed at industry, technology and the economy. In this book, its direction to politics must be the main concern.

In 1961 Michael Shanks, a journalist, published *The Stagnant Society*.[64] He found much to criticise. He believed that an improvement in the material rate of progress was necessary to sustain other values. In a visit to Bulgaria in 1959 he was struck by a similarity with the West: the 'tide of material greed is in fact pulling us all in the same direction.'[65] What the west, and Britain in particular, needed in order to compete, was the injection of a sense of purpose into society. There was great danger in contemplating past glories:

> This is the great psychological danger facing the British people today—that we may bury ourselves under the rose-petals of a vast collective nostalgia, lost in a sweet sad love-affair with our own past.[66]

Radical modernisation was not a partisan outlook in any conventional sense, and it did not fit easily with traditional schools of opinion. Indeed, it was anti-traditional. Perhaps for this reason it has not been recognised as an ideology, and it certainly lacks the full range of ideas found in the great ideologies. However, it was a common way of looking at British politics—it provided a vision and an image of what was going on (not much), and so deserves separate consideration here.

The outlook was, of course, reformist, and some typical proposals are noted later. The proposals were varied, and sometimes similar to those of other outlooks. However, in this case the need for reform derived from the perception of obsolence and stagnation, rather than from any moral critique, or from idealistic concepts. Nor was it merely a conservative process of adjustment; there was too radical an ambience for that. Perhaps it could be characterised as the antithesis of Edmund Burke's view. Instead of distrusting rational schemes of change, it deplored the merely customary, and liked expert innovation.

Viewed in this way, the institutions of British politics looked dignified rather than efficient. The 'Mother of Parliaments is a very weak old lady' wrote Brian Chapman in 1963.[67] 'No other legislature in Europe works under such bad conditions of service and pay, or under rules of procedure which are in practice so heavily weighted in favour of the Government.'[68] And 'The British have discoursed enough about the doctrine of ministerial responsibility, as if this were a source of strength and not, as it is in reality, a source of weakness.'[69] Andrew Shonfield, in *Modern Capitalism*[70] (1965), dealing with the adaptation of government to collectivist circumstances, found

that in Britain intervention was slow: 'There is an abiding
prejudice which sees it as the natural business of government to
react—not to act.'[71] The radical moderniser was essentially an
activist. The much-vaunted British political system was
becoming, for the modernisers, ineffective. In a well-known
article Jack Hayward, Professor of Politics at Hull, wrote:

> Whether we consider the static conservatism of the 1950s or the
> dynamic conservatism of the 1960s, the British political process
> may be said to have triumphed over its purpose. The addiction to
> crisis avoidance has blocked a major road to political
> change.[72]

Criticisms of the British political arrangements were usually
made by comparison. Earlier writers, such as Bagehot and
Dicey had made comparisons, but these were favourable to the
British system. The radical modernisers made frequent
comparisons, and they were rarely favourable. Some aspects
of the American system were admired, such as Congressional
investigative committees, and its general openness was envied.
But it was the practices of West European countries that most
excited the modernisers. The institutions that were admired
illustrate the outlook of these critics. In France the highly-
trained civil service was a prime object of interest: its
recruitment, training, specialisation and *savoir-faire* were
commended. Post-war pessimism gave way, wrote Brian
Chapman

> to the impatience, briskness and efficiency of the young men
> concentrating on influencing the real sources of power in the
> State. They believed in rational planning, expansion, efficiency.
> They were products of the French educational pattern which at
> one and the same time instils a belief that human affairs can be
> better organized by reason rather than instinct, and an intellectual
> arrogance which combines superb self-confidence with a distrust
> of other people's motives.[73]

All of which was lacking in Britain. Another French institution
much envied was the system of administrative law, in complete
contrast to the attitude of Dicey. Andrew Shonfield had a

theory to explain these things:

> The conclusion suggested by the discussion of French economic history was that a set of institutions which were largely pre-capitalist in design could be adapted more readily than others to serve the purposes of the new capitalism, with its large built-in segment of public power, in the second half of the twentieth century.[74]

In practice it was not only French institutions that were noticed. As the decades wore on other European arrangements attracted favour—those of Sweden (open government and the Ombudsman), Italy (the industrial reconstruction institution) Germany (the social market) and Austria (incomes policy) all had their turn.

The radical vision focussed much of its attention on the executive sector of government. Insofar as it used a theory of British politics it was Birch's Whitehall or strong state theory. In a sense the civil service was regarded as out of touch with society: nevertheless its powers of influence and resistance gave it strength. The Fulton Report on the civil service was followed by a book *The Civil Servants*[75] (1980) reiterating the criticisms, by Lord Crowther-Hunt and Peter Kellner. It was subtitled 'an enquiry into Britain's ruling class' and alleged that 'There is a special sense in which the Civil Service reflects the British constitution. Neither is clearly defined in writing: both evolve and change with mood and circumstances.'[76] Brian Chapman, whose book on European civil services was entitled *The Profession of Government*[77] (1959), saw 'wrong decisions' as the cause of British decline. In 1963 he found it 'difficult, looking back on the record of the last ten years to resist the conclusion that it has been marked in many areas of government by a series of wrong decisions.'[78] By and large it was the machinery of executive government that he considered responsible.

In this vision, then, a political system needed ultimately to reach decisions about policy operations—this was what all processes led up to. In Britain as elsewhere the central government took them: but here unprofessional assessments, mistaken perceptions and inadequate analysis led to big errors.

Such an image of the political system is, of course, a bureaucratic (or technocratic) one—decisions are expert calculations, rather than moral choices. Hence the concentration on the civil service and other executive institutions as the key to understanding.

It would be an exaggeration, of course, to say that the central administration was the only target. Business management and trade unions were also attacked. The grounds of attack tended, however, to be the same—lack of professional expertise, and attachment to the good old ways. The unions, wrote Michael Shanks in 1961 'must also recognise that the reservoir of idealism is beginning to dry up. They have become materialist organisations whether they like it or not.'[79] So the solution was similar in all cases—new functionally efficient structures and, especially, more expert management.

The radical quality of the modernisation movement sometimes made it the apparent ally of other schools of thought. But in fact the vision was rarely the same.

For instance, radical modernisers were often bitterly critical of the class system which they perceived in British society and politics. They thought that its rigidities, its snobberies and its false values slowed progress and innovation. Prejudice and nepotism prevented the rise of talented people. Thus modernisation could be the ally of socialism in the desire to change, or destroy social institutions which sustained class barriers, such as the public schools or the City of London.

Nevertheless the intentions were different. Modernisers wanted to open opportunities to all, in the interest of allowing the best to get to the top. They rarely wanted equality in any social or political sense. More typically they favoured a 'meritocracy', a society governed by an elite which really had greater abilities than the rest. Michael Young's book *The Rise of the Meritocracy*[80] published in 1958 was intended as a satire, but its scorn was not in fact perceived by many of its aspirant readers. What they thought was wrong was the survival in Britain of a *traditional* ruling class—which for various historical reasons did not exist in North America, Western Europe or Australia. In practice moreover, the modernisers did not share the solidaristic sympathy with the labour movement characteristic of the class-conflict school. The working class was out-of-date too.

Perhaps, then, the modernisers were allies of the market liberators? Certainly they had attitudes in common—admiration for people who 'did things', the innovators rather than the stabilisers or the moralisers; and a restless search for fluidity and change. The policy recommendations of the radicals were varied, certainly in terms of the other images of British politics. Much of what they proposed was conformable to the main collectivist-arrival school: but it should be done more quickly, since it was already overdue.

In the 1960s writers like Michael Shanks and Andrew Shonfield encouraged the movement towards economic planning, and welcomed its tripartite institutions. A modern technocratic (like the French) planning system was an instrument for economic transformation: respect for the market was old-fashioned and insufficiently purposive. In later decades modernisers tended to accept the arguments about 'pluralist stagnation' and welcomed much of the case for market liberation. The reform of the civil service remained essentially managerialist in inspiration, as with the planners, but private business became the model, and indeed the agent of the modernisation project.

The changes proposed were essentially pragmatic: critics might say merely fashionable. That, however, arose from the nature of the vision. Many of the ideologies around were *old* ideas: capitalism and socialism alike were nineteenth century doctrines. Sophisticated understanding, it was suggested, required that these survivals be transcended. The outlook appealed to professionals and others who felt themselves free of traditional conceptions, or misconceptions. Its lukewarm partisan attachments made it acceptable to those who tired of old conflicts. Modernisation as a concept attracts all those whose activities, in industry, technology or research, are inherently concerned with progressive change. Its values did not clash with those of corporations and other large organisations.

For these reasons it is tempting to associate the modernisers with the wider philosophy which proclaimed the 'end of ideology' or the 'post-industrial society'. These were titles of books[81] by Daniel Bell, an American sociologist. The wider analysis does not concern this book, and it would certainly be wrong to suppose that British modernisers were participating in any profound theoretical debate. Modernisation in many countries and cultures, however, served as a sort of ideology-anti-ideology. Just as conservatives often claim not to be interested in theory, so progressives urged modernisation for its own sake. It was intended to produce economic growth and well-being, of course, but it also avoided—and perhaps diverted attention from—more divisive creeds. Politically, therefore, in Britain as elsewhere, modernisation could serve as a unifying call, a means to consensus as well as dynamism.

This is not to say that the radicals quoted had any such success, in the period here considered. As the years went by they despaired of success. Those who advocated modernisation of government could certainly be associated with the wider and harsher critics of British culture. In *The Collapse of British Power*[82] (1972) and *The Audit of War*[83] (1986) Corelli Barnett, a military historian, deplored the decline of British strength, as evidenced by its operational efficiency as an industrial society. In the latter book he attributed the failure to experience during the Second World War, and to the illusion of success. Consequently there was in post-war years a failure to tackle problems of modernisation.

> The underlying themes of the book lie in the contrast between national pretensions and desires, and national resources; in the clash in the British mind between realism and romanticism, reason and emotion; and above all, in the powerful resistance throughout society to the changes essential for the achievement of maximum success.[84]

In his influential book *English Culture and the Decline of the Industrial Spirit 1850–1980*,[85] Martin Wiener, an American historian, attacks the failure of the British to accept wholeheartedly commercial and industrial values. A chapter is devoted to 'Images and Politics'.[86] The love of the countryside and rejection of urban life by Baldwin, Halifax, Churchill and other Conservative politicians is noted. This led them to reject unbridled capitalism. Similarly churchmen and socialists attacked industrialism, commercialism and above all materialism. The cause of modernisation was thereby given a new slant. Failure to modernise was ascribed not essentially to economic policies or even institutional structures, but to cultural inclinations. The thrusting, materialist young had been frustrated by sentimental attachment to traditional practices, ideals, and scenery. Though both Barnett and Wiener ranged well beyond political life, the images they presented clearly fitted the frame presented by the radical modernisers—British government was resistant to change, excessively concerned with social and moral values, and anti-materialist. Hence their impatience.

The three questions can be posed again. Looked at through the eyes of a moderniser, British political life certainly lacked any sudden transformation. Perhaps it would have been better if it had. Stability and continuity were not virtues. A calamity could do good: 'Rebuilding after massive destruction offers the possibility of modernisation and rationalisation on a scale no country could otherwise envisage.'[87] But they did not foresee a sharp discontinuity in the manner of the Marxists, or even the reverse direction of the market liberators. Acceleration was rather the image they prized. Progress was emphatically defined in material terms, and political and social arrangements were viewed as instruments to this end, more or less efficacious. There was little interest in anything but high politics: the relationship with low politics was that of leaders and led, or government and governed.

6 An Emerging Interpretation

The writings reviewed in previous chapters have created, between them, images of British politics—they have helped to structure people's conceptions of what was happening. However, political imaginations are not filled only with constitutional scenery. They also contain social and historical pictures and in the case of Britain the changing historical view was of particular importance.

Up to the First World War, writers as well as practical politicians generally assumed that the British could choose their own way ahead. Social and political ideas conceived on general political grounds could be put into practice. There were, of course, international rivalries that imposed some constraints. But conservatives and radicals alike assumed that the outside world would not hinder (and indeed might well follow) any reforms that might be undertaken. Wherever general principles (of democracy, liberty, socialism) might lead, then British practice could follow. The realisation of a lesser role in the world altered all that. Political vision became more and more strategic, pragmatic, instrumental. There was a need to check decline, not to achieve new political ideals, but to adapt and correct malformations. The political system itself was regarded as a possible culprit.

There were other lesser shifts of historical vision which affected the perceptions of the political system. As has already been mentioned, the normal understanding of the party system was one of two-party competition, perhaps going back to the seventeenth century. An alternative version of party history however, suggested that there has been since that time a multi-party system in operation. At intervals this system broke through to the parliamentary level, but mostly it was frustrated by the distortions of the electoral arrangements. The facts were the same: it is the interpretation that matters.

There is now a third interpretation: that of Conservative hegemony. In this picture there is one major party, the Conservative, which normally held power. Occasionally (1906, 1945, 1966) another party was able to secure an effective parliamentary majority, but this was rare, and not sustained long enough to disturb the impression of abnormality. If this interpretation is used, then what was significant at any time was the internal situation in the Conservative party.

Another interpretative problem of recent significance concerns the years 1945-74. The depth and extent of the consensus is one issue. But were they years of economic succes or of failure? During this period there was full employment; there was economic growth at a faster rate than at any other time—faster even than in the Victorian period; and on the whole the well-being was more widely spread through the community than at other times. Yet it was also a time when British performance relative to that of other countries became noticeably inferior; and inflation, though moderate for many years, persistently tended to rise. So there is a sharply divided assessment of the merits of the period, which colours the views taken of the political arrangements of the time.

A glance at the whole period covered in this book, from the mid-nineteenth century onwards, shows a trend from rather limited discourses on 'the constitution' to attempts to describe the 'political system', at best British society in its political aspect. The turning point comes after the Second World War, and is connected with the growth of academic political science and American intellectual influence.

A longer and more searching look shows that this is not entirely the case. Virtually every generation of writers considers its predecessors to have been excessively narrow and formal, and claims to be introducing a new realism into the subject. Mill considered what seemed the basic question, what form of society could sustain representative government; Bagehot insisted that he offered a realistic account, above all, of how things actually were; Dicey not only described conventions as well as written law, but stipulated a place for political theory beyond that. The change is not in realism, but in what is held to constitute reality.

Bagehot, Low, Muir and Laski were essentially brilliant essayists. Their accounts, even if in textbook form, lived by the persuasiveness of their sketches. They wrote from knowledge but their eminence was a matter of inspiration. From the beginning of the century, however, there emerged a new empiricism, from Ostrogorski, Wallas and Lowell onwards. It lapsed until the post-1945 years. The lawyer Jennings softened the distinction between law and politics in his passive volumes. Between the wars it was left to Ramsay Muir to discover the ruling functions of civil servants and (to his dismay) of interest groups.

In the 1950s and 1960s the vision did shift and new behaviouristic analyses were offered, allegedly of course more realistic, and certainly better researched. But the concentration on elections, parties, groups and communications was not all gain. Little was heard about the legal system—it was too 'formal'. Local government became a specialised subject, not a countervailing force in the polity. Scotland, Wales and Northern Ireland were only noticed by scholars after the devolution crisis. Little was written about the police until the 1970s, and less about the armed forces, though few would have thought to give a political account of any foreign country without discussing the role of the military.

In the older descriptive texts of the pre-1939 period some note was taken of these matters—A.L. Lowell in 1908 gave a full account of local government, education (including universities), the Church and the free churches, the courts of law, the central departments and the Crown.[1] Laski in 1938 included the House of Lords, the judiciary and the monarchy.[2] By the 1970s it seemed that the role of interest groups, of the permanent civil service, of quangos, of the forces and of the judiciary made the political process very complex.[3] Policy-making had entered a post-parliamentary era. Dicey's assurance that the electorate was the political sovereign and that its will was sure to prevail was becoming remote.[4] In the 1980s however, the determined management of central power, once a Government was elected, made these obstacles look less formidable. If the power of Dicey's electorate was still lost, it was lost in the electoral system.

CONSENSUS AND CLEAVAGE

It has been suggested in earlier chapters that the 1945-74 period in British politics was one of consensus—a time when disagreement did not challenge major areas of policy. This proposition needs to be explained and defended. It does not mean that there were no differences, even in the most consensual matters. It does not mean that there were no active and effective political groups, outside any consensus. Nor does it mean that the moral principles and the social interests behind the policy applications were not widely divergent. Throughout the period party rivalry and bitter argument flourished.

Nevertheless it can be asserted that, from the later years of the second world war until 1974 there was a set of attitudes shared between most of the influential politicians: (i) support for foreign and defence policies which made Britain an important member of the NATO alliance; (ii) support in the 1950s and 1960s for policies which granted independence to most colonies; (iii) support for Keynesian economic management, designed to maintain full employment and to promote economic growth; (iv) support for a mixed economy in which some industries remained in state ownership, managed by public corporations, while the major part of industry was not nationalised; (v) the maintenance of a range of social welfare services, including the National Health Service; (vi) the development of systems of town planning, regional economic subsidies, and until the 1970s building new towns; (vii) the continuance of agricultural subsidies, until they were replaced by the EEC levy system in the 1970s. There were also measures of agreement in other matters: comprehensive schools for example, though pressed by the Labour Party, were in fact also promoted by other parties. The list could be extended.

It is also part of this view that the consensus broke down in the 1970s, and that wider disagreement has resulted in the polarisation of British politics. Certainly in many matters there has emerged a much wider gap. The most important of these was the change in methods of economic management after 1979, that is suspension of Keynesian demand management and of priority given to full employment. This switch in priorities was undoubtedly divisive. There was also in the 1980s a programme of privatisation of industrial (and other) governmental activities, and though this was apparently fundamental—on the capitalist/socialist view of political division—it attracted less than determined opposition.

Consensus does not and did not mean unanimity. There were in existence very deep cleavages on many of these issues: the point was that they did not force themselves on to those who determined policy. There was a left wing, within the Labour party and beyond, which asserted strong Marxist policies of state ownership and anti-NATO foreign policies. There was a market-oriented economic right which rejected Keynesian and welfare policies. But the split was not between the parties, and did not have much effect on the rival leaderships. There was also social cleavage. Class voting was common, and in Britain class difference deeply penetrated education, commerce and social activities. But these are not the issues. The truth is that there was a relatively high degree of political consensus at the policy-making level between the 1940s and the 1970s.

Bearing in mind these and other evaluations of the post-1945 period, an attempt can now be made the review the five general views of the political system—the widespread notion of collectivist arrival; conservative scepticism and market liberation; class struggle and radical modernisation. Though ideological sympathies were always hovering in the background, these images of the system were not in themselves ideologies, nor did they fit any particular classification of ideologies. They were (and are) convenient for the present purpose—that is, for distinguishing between different points of vantage on the political scene: different interpretations.

A strength of the collectivist arrival view was its manifest congruence with major developments. It was plainly in tune with the growth of big organisations, governmental and other-wise. But this fit was also the source of a weakness—a tendency to accept what was happening as necessary and even desirable. The way of the world had no doubt to be coped with somehow; but it was not desirable to be uncritical. It accepted, even welcomed, the democracy of the electoral process— indeed, it took this process to be the force bringing change. It assumed realistically enough that active politicians were power-hungry. Therefore they sought not only to provide what the power-granting electorate wanted, material well-being, but they sought to obtain the credit for it. The system was not designed; rather it emerged. It was responsive. The formal institutions might be in need of reform, but the operative organisations—the competitive parties and the pressure groups—were flexible instruments of fluctuating demands. Hence it seemed probable that the system had built into it the means of adaptation.

The variants tended of course, to complicate the simple picture. In particular the 'two languages' of liberal elections and strong central government seemed to provide a better image at the end of the period than they had earlier. The economic crisis of the 1970s and the alleged 'overload' turned into a crisis for the collectivist interpretation of the political system. Its characteristic methods of institutional creation (such as quangos) and of negotiations with interests were regarded (perhaps wrongly) as no longer capable of expansion. Moreover, the vision of party competition proved illusory— the Labour party was too weak a vessel to sustain the role of effective adversary, since it failed to win reliable majorities in 1974, and weakened further thereafter.

The appeal of conservative scepticism lay in the detached prospect of actuality which it took. The central theme—of a traditional governing power—cannot have been far wrong judged by the test of survival. Executive power prevailed in Britain in 1988 as it did in 1945. The scepticism about the other developments may also have been true: at any rate in 1988 many of them seemed less secure and the 'oscillation' thesis had achieved a certain plausibility.[5]

Nevertheless, the detachment of this school had its costs. No doubt if a long enough view is taken, things will change. The follies of reformers often provide easy targets, but their efforts also determine the shape of change. Attempting to understand the intimations of past experience may lead not to wise statesmanship but to confusion and indecision—the lessons of history are numerous, and no one knows for sure which are relevant. In the practical politics of the 1970s and 1980s there were problems for those of this outlook, for the tradition in Britain had become one of widespread State provision, which they distrusted, and so their inclinations were to support drastic changes. 'Radical conservatism is a contradiction in terms' said Lord Alport in the Lords in 1987;[6] and this surely epitomises a dilemma for this interpretation.

Market liberation faced no such problem. It was, in the circumstances of the post-war years, essentially a critical vision. It distrusted so much of the development in that period that its institutional judgements were generally negative. The merits of the outlook lay in its consistency and its logic. Like other radical ideals, however, it fell into difficulties when turned to practical operations, and to a process of piecemeal change. For example, criticism of the distortive effects of pressure groups might lead to attempts to minimise their influence. But since they could not be eliminated entirely, what resulted was merely a new pattern of influence, favouring (for example) bankers more and trade unionists less. The idealism of this outlook, based on radical individualism, looked to a sort of groupless utopia which was as absurd as a guide to political practicality as was its counterpart 'full communism'. The commonest proposition for governmental reform from this point of view lay in some form of permanent constitutional law, but again as a matter of practicality no move was made.

It did not require very much penetration to see evidence of class conflict in the political events of British politics in this (or any) period. It required more confidence however, to use this phenomenon as the prime explanatory guide. The idea of containment was realistic enough. Few governments could deny that their policies were framed to ensure their continuance in office, and to avoid provoking a revolution. At this level it was hard to demur. But containment, suspiciously, could be used retrospectively to explain any kind of policy. After the event it could be seen that welfare policies contained post-war discontent, and later that tax-cutting policies contained popular resentment. The problem was in predicting which policies would be used to contain future development. Worse, whatever they were, they could be described as forms of containment. Here, surely, was a truism, not an explanation.

The more sophisticated forms of class analysis had more to offer; but again there was a suspicion that the key concepts (of class, of interest) could be defined so flexibly as to fit almost anything. It was, however, a merit or at any rate a potential merit, of this outlook that it looked out more widely than others. The breadth of vision beyond conventional political phenomena may have made the data unmanageable and the theories wildly speculative, but at least it encouraged exploration.

Radical modernisation had perhaps a similar virtue in that it looked beyond Britain more than other outlooks. On the other hand, the comparisons were rarely systematic and sustained. Until the later explorations of cultural factors, the outlook lacked much depth of analysis. Modernisation is the natural creed of the young and the ambitious. When the perception of decline grew, it became more and more apposite to urge that old institutions and customary procedures had something wrong with them somewhere. This outlook was capable of joining with others, provided that rapid change was envisaged, and later in the chapter more is said about its eventual fruition.

Three questions have been asked at intervals through the book about the different viewpoints, in order to show some similarities and differences.

The distinction between 'high' and 'low' politics can be understood in many ways. In their book *High and Low Politics in Modern Britain*[7] (1983) Bentley and Stevenson include essays on a variety of themes. Unfortunately the only definition, offered by José Harris,[8] allows 'high politics' to include types of activity so general (anything which involves a real contest over the distribution of power) as to obliterate the value of the distinction. One way of interpreting high and low is to make them much the same as centre and periphery. In this view high politics are matters which concern the central government in London: low politics are dealt with by quangos, regions and localities. Or high may mean elite affairs; and low, matters for the masses. Again, high politics can refer to the crucial issues of power, the things that really matter; while consequently low politics are affairs of lesser importance.

Now there is some obvious congruence about these definitions. The rise of democracy in the late nineteenth century caused alarm because it was thought that the practices of high politics could not be sustained: there was relief in the decades that followed when this seemed not to be the case. All the major schools of thought have some distinction which approximates to a high/low division, though the market liberators care little for it, and some Marxists and radical democrats imagine that it can be ended. The nature of the relationship between the high level of politics and low varies. In some visions (Tories, technocratic modernisers, Leninists) the essential business of elite politicians is to govern—that is to manage the turbulent low life of mass politics. In other visions (pluralist, liberal) the movements of unsophisticated people are (and should be) the determinants of the actions of active and informed ruling groups. For some, again, the sphere of high politics is very small (the inner Cabinet, say); while others may see it as extending to most of the articulate public.

The vision of politics may be one of essential continuity, or it may be marked by some sharp break. Such a critical shock may be in the past, or envisaged in the future. In Britain, the continuity (at least since the seventeenth century) was often remarked. Some, incredibly, traced it back to the pre-Norman unification of England. In the post-war years, continuity seemed the main theme in most visions: political and economic arrangements had evolved, and there was no real prospect of a cataclysm. Major changes (loss of empire, entry to the EEC) were brought about without domestic upheaval. The major policy switches were those of 1945 and 1979, and these were occasioned by entirely constitutional elections. Two ideologies, free market radicalism and Marxism, did advocate dramatic breaks with the past. The 1980s saw one of these gain influence, and it was significant that its propogators found themselves frequently repudiating past developments, even those emanating from the same party.

The third question concerned the nature of political progress. What were the desired futures? Over the period since the nineteenth century the criterion of material wellbeing became increasingly dominant. For one reason, ways of measuring it (by income per head, for example) became practicable. There were two other major ideals, rivals at some stages. One was obviously national power—expressed at first in terms of imperial expansion, later as ability to influence world events, or at least European events. The early forms became impracticable, and later national prestige became both an expression of and a means towards economic prosperity. The third standard of progress—movement towards a better form of society, or some form of social justice—was prevalent in mid-century, but again became confused or subsumed, in general political life, with material affluence. Of course this is not to suggest that any of these ideas lost their places in sophisticated political discussion, or that in practice there was anything but a shifting amalgam of values and interests in play in political life. No doubt the polity had no ultimate destiny, as some conservative sceptics pointed out. Nevertheless at the level of operative ideas economic gained increasingly at the expense of social or political achievement. Even liberty, the queen of all political virtue, was gratifyingly related to welfare as both cause and effect. Political institutions therefore were commonly judged in this light.

BETWEEN THE LINES

In this book the interpretations and images discussed have been those created by reputable authors. These writers interpret what they observe; and their interpretations become operative concepts and images. Even at this quality level of interpretation—that is, without discussing mass or populist impressions—it is nevertheless necessary to say something about what is implicit rather than explicit.

The languages in which politics is discussed are largely figurative. No doubt there are specific terms that have so long lost sight of their derivations that they are nothing but political. Nevertheless political language—of explanation as well as of rhetoric—need something more. Words that will communicate effectively are needed. Thus in the middle ages and afterwards the vocabulary was largely that of the human body. Kings and other rulers were heads, and the rest fitted less exalted organs. This language may not have been intended literally; nevertheless it was convenient because it was a familiar form of discourse.

As noted in Chapter 1, the common terminology is now mechanical. Such words as 'power', 'structure', 'framework', 'machinery' (of government), 'pressure', 'control', 'steering' (the economy) and so on are used. Ordinary political terms which have become literal (legislature, election, govern) make a start, but naturally and inevitably they are supplemented freely by whatever seems expressive from other vocabularies. In this book visual terms (image, picture, focus) and musical terms (themes) have been used, and other are possible. Perhaps, as computer terminology enters common parlance, it will be used for political purposes—indeed, a 'software society' where services not manufacturing predominate has already been proclaimed.

The value of such developments is obvious—they discourage rigidity. The danger is that from time to time their metaphorical nature is unrecognised, and they are taken near-literally. Governmental bodies do not actually operate with the certainties of machines; economies cannot really be steered; group sanctions do not have the constancy of pressure. Power, the most impressive of these terms, is a causal concept in politics as in mechanics (action A brings about effect B), but in politics it is commonly believed to be applied downwards only (another physical metaphor). 'Basis' is used so frequently that the physical relationship has been forgotten.

One common practice deserves particular note, in the context of this study. Since the Second World War it has become usual to divide economies into a 'public sector' and a 'private sector'. The economists no doubt need these terms. They have also developed into regular political descriptions, and this is less easy to justify. The 'private sector' includes not only all individuals and their households, but business concerns large and small (if they are not publicly owned), and many independent institutions, associations, charities and—though they scarcely seem aware of it—trade unions. The 'public sector' contains, besides the central government, all public enterprises, local authorities and their services, law courts, armed forces, and quangos.

What is elusive about the usage is the supposition (and the origin of the supposition) that this sector comprises a harmonious unity. In many operative conceptions now in Britain it is equivalent to 'the state'. At all events it is supposed to be susceptible of central control, at least for economic purposes. The relevance of all this in the present context is, of course, the image of political society that has been created by the infiltration of this innocent terminology. The crude dichotomy that is implied is surely unjustified; yet for much analysis and controversy—even at sophisticated levels—little more is offered.

There are other filters affecting the picture in the lens, besides those of language. All political societies depend on myth to some degree, and the British are far from exceptional. Mostly these are historical myths, and necessarily lay great stress on past victories and not on past defeats. Two such myths relevant to the themes already discussed, are the 'forward march of labour' and the 'road to serfdom'. Both these images buttress ideologies as well as colour perceptions of what is, or is not, the current political system. To assert that they are mythological is only to say that they will not stand up to close historical examination. Like most myths, however, they have some basis in reality: they are not wholly untrue. At a certain level of broad generalisation they can be persuasive. It is comforting to have the tide of history with you, even if (as with the road to serfdom) it was in ebb for a hundred years or so.

However, though all systems need myths, they can be evaluated. In 1984 Stuart Walkland and Andrew Gamble wrote that they

> would agree that every political society, to exist at all, needs some degree of consensus, more often than not based on myth, and fortified by ritual. As Pareto observed both ritual and myth play a fundamental role in legitimation. But the myths produced by the post-war British system have been economically damaging and have impeded the development of the conditions needed for economic growth.[9]

Few post-1945 writers on British politics mention ritual, let alone analyse it. Nor is there any well-known discussion of British myths, except insofar as they are sometimes linked with that embracing concept, political culture. There is rarely any chapter in the texts on the monarchy nowadays, and much of what is written is disparaging—though it could be said that the monarchy is the most successful British political institution of the century, having contributed most in terms of stability, unity and popularity. It plays no part in the main constitutional pictures, except that of conservative scepticism, where it is revered but not analysed. Ritual and myth flourish elsewhere, notably in election procedures and in Parliament. They are often the bugbear of reformers, but even so get little attention. Perhaps the trouble is that myth is hard to fit into the mechanistic modes of description that are most convenient and prevalent.

Or, alternatively, it may be thought that the decline of deference justifies the neglect of these factors. Certainly deference, and the acceptance of hierarchy as normal, was from Bagehot the prime non-rational factor included in most descriptions of the British system. In 1956 Edward Shils, the American sociologist, published *The Torment of Secrecy*[10] in the wake of the McCarthyite pressures in the United States. He contrasted the continuing deference and respect for privacy in Britain with the populism and fear of secrecy in the United States, on the whole to the detriment of the United States:

> Through the spirit of privacy, the deferential attitude towards government is reinforced. If anybody in Britain would have grounds to feel that the ruling group was secretive, it would be the lower and middle classes, who are so excluded from 'inside' knowledge. Much more is withheld in Britain than America from the scrutiny of the public. Yet the ruling classes in Great Britain are respected, and they are entitled, in the eyes of the mass of the population (lower middle class and working class, rural and urban) to possess their secrets as long as they are not obviously harming anyone. Thus the circle is turned, and an equilibrium of secrecy, privacy, and publicity kept stable.[11]

Since 1956 this equilibrium has departed. Nothing could better mark the change in the British system over thirty years than the passionate distrust of inner-circle politics which developed from the 1960s. No great opening of the secrecy was actually achieved by the 1980s, but the trust had gone.

But even if this sort of respect has gone, other factors remain. Indeed, the decline of deference is in some ways both cause and effect of the perceived national crisis.

Another American, Richard Hofstadter, published in 1966 a book entitled *The Paranoid Style in American Politics.*[12] There is a paranoid style in British politics too. On the left strange fears and conspiracies are believed, concocted behind a secret constitution; and on the right subversives of many sorts, 'enemies within', are expected to triumph every hour. But more characteristic of the British way is what might be called the masochistic style. Rapturous applause is likely to greet the call 'Hard choices have to be made.' It is true that the hard choices are more attractive in the abstract than in the particular, and that the worst consequences are deserved by others. Opinion polls consistently show, however, that people rate the ability of leaders to take tough unpopular decisions very highly. Both Conservative and Labour leaders are admired for crushing rebellions within their own parties. It is not suggested of course, that in the event the British really enjoy hard times: the recurrent phenomenon lies in the style of rhetoric rather than the policy outcomes.

THE EMERGING SCENE

So far this book has dealt with the existing pictures of the system. There is always change, as the various accounts have revealed, and new visions begin to form in the fog.

It is tempting to try to look further. In the 1980s the Prime Minister gave her name to a new ideology, Thatcherism. There are many excellent accounts of this phenomenon, and there is no point in trying to add to them here.[13] The point is merely to note how far this new detail adds to the picture.

In the terms already used in this book, Thatcherism is a combi-nation of two themes: a preference for market-liberation policies with a determined tory grip on authority. Market-liberation as such could be linked with decentralised administration, or with an internationalist philosophy, but it is not. Andrew Gamble's title *The Free Economy and the Strong State* (1988) sums it up.[14] What Thatcherism does not contain is the strategic pragmatism that was the prime characteristic of Conservatives in Britain for nearly two hundred years, after the eloquent denunciations of rationalism by Edmund Burke.

Now the classic analysts of the British system in the 1960s cannot be blamed for not taking into account such an outlook. It was not there. The elements of which it is composed might have been discerned, but the full image was not formed. So their visions were not faulty. Similarly it is not to be expected that current notions will fare any better in the matter of prediction.

What can be attempted, however, is to delineate certain features of the present situation that deserve more emphasis. Some factors are obvious, and they are none the less important for that. Some others may be so obvious that they are taken for granted. In these cases the task is to make explicit what is assumed. It is not quite putting into words what everyone knows already: it is rather to assert the significance of what might be thought commonplace.

From this standpoint it is necessary to consider the state of British nationalism. The tendency of writers on British politics to 'leave out' certain topics for decades or more has been noted—the armed forces and the judicial system for example. When nationalism was brought into view in the 1960s and 1970s it was sub-state nationalism—Scots and Welsh nationalism. Even now the nationalism of the English or the British is rarely made clear. It is too omnipresent to be noticed; there are too many trees to see the wood.

In 1956 Edward Shils tried. He observed that:

Although the British and the official spokesman of their corporate institutions are much afflicted with national conceit, on the whole they are less preoccupied with the symbols of nation and of national unity than some of the more vociferous Americans. Those who are so preoccupied get less of a hearing and are less influential. On ceremonial occasions, the national symbols are less frequently invoked and less intensely invoked in Great

Britain than in America. In the United States a trade or professional association, being addressed at a conference, is more likely to learn about the threat of Communism and the needs of national defense. In Great Britain this is less likely to be so. It is not that there are not in all political positions in Great Britain, hyper-patriots who refer everything they discuss to a British standard and find it wanting. There are many Englishmen, especially since the war, who have Britain on their minds over all else. But they do not, on the surface at least, seem to be defending themselves from external attack. British jingoism does not seem to be in such need of the internal homogeneity of society as its American counterpart. American hyper-patriotism seems always to call for loyalty, maximum loyalty, while British national conceit is capable of being unworried by the internal heterogeneity of British society. The British phenomenon is directed towards foreigners; the American towards other Americans as well as foreigners.[15]

Things have changed, in Britain at any rate.

Three aspects of British national self-regard are relevant to the present question, of how the country sees its system of government. First, its scope; secondly, its style; and thirdly its intensity.

The scope of British nationalism has obviously been transformed by post-war events. The bizarre practice of calling the UK Parliament the Imperial Parliament has long disappeared, and more important there have been intermittent pressures for national devolution within the kingdom. Immigration has emphasised the problems of ethnic pluralism. The range of what British nationalists are being nationalist about has thus been modified. Notoriously, passions can still be aroused about remote islands, but there are fewer such places. But the worries about internal heterogeneity have become much greater than Shils observed. In these circum-stances the celebrated unitary nature of the British constitution must have become less secure. On the one hand, unity and a single system can be seen as a force for cementing national cohesion in the face of potential fragmentation; on the other hand, it can be regarded as unrealistic in the new social circumstances.

The style of British nationalism used to be self-confident and detached. Though never insular (the existence of a world-wide empire prevented that) the British tended to be less than European. The dominant political ideologies in Britain were non-dogmatic—the conservatism of cautious adaptation; the new liberalism of piecemeal state involvement; and Fabian gradualist socialism all had a practical inclination. Many professed to be suspicious of grand theory ('foreign doctrines'), though they were unconscious carriers of inchoate theories in fact. There was a national prejudice at work. If these ideas were prevalent, however illusory, then a system based on party conflict and alternation in office could work: one could take over from another in an orderly way, and moral conflict and policy argument could exist within a continuous national tradition. Polarisation threatens this style. Whatever happened to the British system? ask foreign commentators.[16]

These factors affect the quality of nationalism. It is hard to judge this matter, but the nationalism of decline seems to be of a more intense and desperate nature than that of the time of expansion and apparent success. All nationalisms are in competition with one another, that is their danger. The ways of rating national achievement have increased, especially in economic matters, and many new arenas in sport and the arts have been created, in which victory is possible but defeat more likely. In these circumstances there is a constant pressure for achievement in national terms. The nation finds itself the embodiment of more and more types of human aspiration. These changes apply to all nations; for the British whose historical development puts them into a phase in which they can no longer match their previous eminence, the stress is much greater.

Hence the new factor in the political landscape, since the 1950s—the dominance of the 'state of Britain' question. Its essentials may be once more re-iterated.

Of course, the fact of decline really shaped the change. Awareness, however, was an additional matter. It was the realisation of decline that most affected the image of the system. This awareness came later than the fact. In the 1860s Bagehot assumed Britain to be a 'first-rate nation'. It was undoubtedly a great power. Most significant perhaps was the assumption of success. The British constitution was one of the world's great political systems, to be admired as well as analysed. It was plausible to argue that it was one of the causes of Britain's greatness. In the evolution of the previous three hundred years this was true: the spread of British political philosophies was accompanied by the attempted imitation of British institutions.

Now the decline problem has become the main feature of political concern, and philosophies and policies come to be treated as instruments to secure revival. Its precedence has scarcely wavered, though there have been two special episodes in the story. The first episode was in the late 1950s and early 1960s, after the Suez adventure had shown the weakness of Britain's international position. Though prosperity was rising, the rate of growth in Britain was slower than that of similar industrial countries. Hence policy initiatives such as voluntary economic planning and membership of the EEC were launched; and—almost as important for the political scene—a spate of books and other writings appeared on these and similar issues. The second episode followed in the 1970s and 1980s, when market liberation policies were presented as leading to the 'rebirth of Britain'.[17]

So the flourishing five themes of interpretation began to be transformed by the new emphasis. It was the radical modernisers who gained most: their proposals, though often imitative, were put forward as Britain-saving devices. The market liberators rode this horse successfully in the 1980s, though they had gained nothing in the 1960s. The believers in class struggle adapted well enough—the specific British weakness was attributable to the peculiar strength of finance capital or the incomplete social transformation—the fecundity of the genre was not destroyed. Conservative sceptics reserved their scepticism: provided that the right chords in the traditional manner of behaviour could be struck, all might be well. The great collectivist-arrival school was embarrassed, but not defeated. Decline was not what they expected. Adaptation to electoral demands, the main engine of change, had to be modified by the needs of international rivalry—but as the electorate's mood responded to the British crisis, this could be accommodated. The electorate wanted Britain to win, even if many of them lost their jobs in the process. And the collectivists noted that, even with a drive towards market freedom, new quangos appeared, new regulatory bodies were necessary and meso-corporatism was still there.

A new nationalism, the nationalism of decline, thus took its place in the foreground.

A second theme in the emerging scene of British politics was a new managerialism. It was more explicit than the new nationalism, because it was less completely accepted. Though its basic assumptions were very widely acknowledged, its more radical assertions caused open controversy, and so the outlook was brought into political view.

The twentieth-century tendency to describe social affairs by mechanical metaphors has already been noted, and this was part of the story. The view that British politics was in need of radical modernisation was another element in the new construction, though it will be seen that nearly all the main interpretations of the post-war period made a contribution.

The main causal factor in the development was the growth of formal organisations; hence there was a greater level of participation in organisational life; and hence there was a more common acceptance of organisational assumptions. The main organisations in question were business concerns (where the assumptions are held most fervently), but other governmental and non-governmental bodies were all involved. There had been of course, business concerns and other bodies at all times but apart from military formations they had usually been smaller and less predominant in society; and were in any case less tightly controlled. What was politically crucial was the normality. As people came to think that this was how things were normally arranged, then other relationships became strange, unusual and perhaps slightly absurd or old-fashioned.

The arrangements of organisational life thus generated a political style. It was possibly a bastard style. Some writers in political science refused to accept the legitimacy of 'private government' in firms, churches, trade unions and so on as authentic politics. It is not necessary to argue this issue here—though many of these purists seemed to accept the resemblances as at least quasi-political. However, people learn from their own experiences; and they carry over thought patterns they acquire in one part of their lives into others. Not doubt it is a process fraught with confusion, and liable to many limitations. But this seemed to be happening in Britain in respect of organisational life. It was relevant of course that the habits were picked up most rapidly by the political élite. The skills of administration, market research, and articulate expression which were used in organisations were also helpful in politics, and so common practices led to common frames of reference, and they were both easily transmitted.

The influence of one form of life on another was accepted without much question in earlier political periods. The ideas immanent in religions were reflected in the governments of all societies from the earliest to the present. To give a specific example, in Britain the practices of nonconformist churches in their internal affairs encouraged ideas which were carried into the Liberal party and into the trade unions. From these origins the Labour party derived some of its principles and many of its problems.

A preliminary explanation of the managerialist outlook can be made by contrasting some of its terms, with those of the more customary outlook—at least, with what were the customary terms in mid-century. Both sets of concepts were fundamentally political, in the way they were coming to be used. So the older language is termed 'representational' after one of its key concepts. It owed much to liberal theory but there were other influences in practice. Indeed, both lists reflect operational politics rather than philosophic ideas.

Representational concepts	*Managerialist concepts*
Ideals	Objectives
Representation	Research and consultation
Will, opinion	Facts, data
Votes	Behaviour
Discussion, debate	Analysis
Authority	Right to manage
Responsibility	Accountability
Pressure	Obstacles, constraints
Values	Priorities
Reform	Success
Legitimacy	Efficiency

It is not suggested that the terms are exact substitutes or translations. Indeed, how could they be? The point is that managerialist notions provide a systematic way of looking at the world—as a sort of magnification of the affairs of lesser entities. Though no organisation (by definition) is comparable in nature with 'great societies', many are very large and embracing, hence their impact on the imagination. The expressions listed rather present a set of alternatives to the representational set. Thus, if a political activist were to talk of ideals, a managerialist would want to formulate objectives. Instead of seeking to make policy by representational systems to reflect people's wishes, managerialists instigate research; and instead of debate and discussion, a rigorous analysis of the data is put forward as the basis for action. And so with other concepts. The list could be extended.

The managerialist style is more immediately operational than is the representational. That is one source of its strength. The representational style does provide a sequence of cause and effect by which political change can be brought about—either in Dicey's model whereby the electorate was an effective sovereign, or in the more complex post-1945 model whereby party competition and pressure led to governmental response. But they proved very hit-and-miss processes. In firms and other organised bodies the systems of decision-making and of implementation were (ostensibly) more direct and more viable. So an attraction in using this family of concepts lay in its promise of effectiveness.

It must be emphasised at this point that what is being discussed in this chapter is the extension of such notions into the political system, *not* merely their use within executive government. There are now innumerable governmental organisations, in Britain as elsewhere. These bodies—departments, local authorities, military formations, quangos—are part of the natural habitat of organisational ideas. Their use, however, is spreading from this base.

The public corporations which ran nationalised industries were always completely managerial. The National Health Service had from 1946 embodied a system of representation of interests that was quasi-political. The reforms of the 1970s and 1980s reduced these arrangements in favour of managerial decision-making. In 1985, universities, which hitherto had been understood to be self-governing and self-orienting institutions, were enjoined in the Jarratt report[18] to reorganise themselves, reduce committee work and put control in the hands of the chief executive; and concurrently to be recast as a coherent national system. Reforms pressed on the civil service in this period all stressed 'management' as distinct from administration or even policy preparation.

Now, taken singly, any of these can be regarded as proper objects of organisational logic, and its practical consequences. Taken together, and with other similar developments they indicate a spreading area of formal organisation. With more and more parts taking up the philosophy, then its application to the whole becomes more customary, more like commonsense. But even these extensions do not carry the matter far enough. Ordinary politicians began to talk, at times, this way. It is political understanding itself that is in question.

The concept that takes the new image out of the structured system into wider realms is that of efficiency. There has been concern about British 'national efficiency' since the mid-nineteenth century,[19] and as noted the perceived decline of Britain has led to searches, ever more agonised, for its determinants. 'Inefficiency' is the general concept into which state-of-Britain diagnoses are fitted. In origin the term derives from mechanics and economics, and the burgeoning of macro-economic statistics after 1941 made relevant national computations feasible. It is the widespread belief that the country *as a whole*—the society in some complete sense—ought to become more efficient that gives 'efficiency' its pretensions to political status.

Just as crises of confidence have suffused political life since 1960, so has the criterion of efficiency been applied in wider and wider contexts. In order to advance national prestige, it is thought necessary to reform the organisation of such activities as education, sport and the arts. Other organisational concepts follow that of efficiency, for without their aid ('analysis') how is improvement to be brought about? And beyond efficiency—the purpose of the efficiency—lurks the bitch-goddess[20] herself.

The differences between the two forms in practice should not be exaggerated. It is possible to stress the political nature of management. Ted Stephenson's book, *Management: a Political Activity*[21] (1985) 'presents the view that management is substantially a political activity, based on power and characterised by conflict.'[22] and also he notes that 'Management, like politics, is concerned with coping with differences.'[23]

This is only an example. In fact the literature of management and of organisation theory is replete with works on the human dimensions, on how people matter, on appreciating the real world, on informal relations and many similar matters. There is no suggestion that the subject is any less sensitive or aware than other political studies, which as pointed out are themselves full of mechanistic expressions. The difference does not lie in this direction. The contrast is in the degree of cohesion, of apparent purposiveness, and the assumptions about the extent to which arrangements should be directed to common ends, usually by some central or superior authority.

Perhaps it all really depends on the matter of objectives. They are one of the defining characteristics of organisations: that is, an organisation is distinguished from other human groupings by having definable objectives. In the managerialist mode little progress can be made until objectives are clarified. It may be noted, on the side, that the call to 'formulate objectives' though necessary is often a deceptive move in the organisational world. If objectives are not already clear it may well be because they are truly and genuinely vague, or multiple, or in flux. Formulating objectives is a function of practicality; they are not self-legitimating, and consent to them may not be enduring. The effect is to elevate 'ends' to prior importance, and to legitimate means (or putative means) to these ends. They are incurably rationalistic.

Much has been heard, in recent decades, about a 'right to manage'. It sounds suspiciously like a 'right to rule', and surely cannot be a human right—it occurs in no declarations, and it cannot be universalised. Nevertheless for managers it is more than a craving for power—it embodies a need to practice their art. If all their knowledge and expertise ends in frustration, they seek remedies which appear to them as liberations. Such urges are easily transferred to state activities, with formidable consequences.

To return to present purposes, however, the need is to understand these developments as they affect the image of the political system. A two-language model is possible. In the 1960s Anthony Birch proposed that British politics could be described in two ways (in liberal language and in Whitehall language). A similar duality may now be arising between representational language and managerial language. The two co-exist, and they are not exclusive.

Nevertheless, they are not entirely compatible. The representative language, though owing much to liberal ideas, is not in fact so simple—most of the five interpretations are involved in it. The two languages lead to strong differences of emphasis in practice. For example, ideals are unattainable, but objectives are supposed to be practicable. In the managerialist view, opinions are no substitute for hard facts: in the representational model, opinion, will, *volonté* is the supreme criterion of policy. Their democratic orientation is therefore quite different. Representational systems are not always entirely democratic, or indeed very democratic at all in the more demanding senses of that flexible concept. But they rely in the main on 'political' activity—voting, discussing, expressing views, wheeling and dealing. Managerialism takes account of what people want by researching it—by survey, by reviewing behaviour, by testing responses. The representational mode looks strongly (though not exclusively) to the public arena for its key procedures. Managerialism prefers the limited methods of small committees and measurable impartial criteria.

In the end, of course, managerialism by itself is sterile as a political ideology. Efficiency is related only to means, not ends. It turns on the relationship between input (of resources) and output. Output of what? Within organisations, objectives can be formulated, as discussed. But what are the objects of society at large? Surely here the outlook reveals its emptiness, and traditional political ideologies come into their own?

In Britain, the ideology that fills the gap is the one just discussed—nationalism. The two underlying beliefs are linked. A regular habit of nationalism is to pair with another ideology—thus in the world there are radical nationalists, socialist nationalist, conservative nationalists, religious nationalists. The objective of managerialism in Britain is to achieve national success—prestige, power, influence, respect.

'Managerial nationalism' therefore looks like the most suitable expression to encapsulate this emerging interpretation of the British political system. It still runs alongside other interpretations, market, collectivist and conservative. It is capable, however, of gaining popularity and influence against them. More people, that is to say, will see the political system in this way, and judge it accordingly. If the vision becomes even more common, it will lead to reform campaigns, to adapt the system to its norms. For a time at any rate (like other nostrums) it may seem to offer a way out of decline.

An alternative expression would be 'technocratic nationalism', and in the strict sense of technocratic might be justifiable. However in common parlance 'technocratic' has been associated with 'high technology' which in turn has been narrowed to computer electronics and the like. This is not the issue, and so technocratic has become a misleading term. 'Managerial' catches the flavour better—skilled deployment of structures and resources from the top—and so is the preferable adjective.

Doubtless managerial nationalism has not yet arrived, fully-fledged, as a sixth interpretation, standing alongside the five described earlier. Certainly it lacks the focus on the actual political system that some of them embody. It nevertheless encourages attitudes towards that system, even if these are not yet constitutive of a well-formed alternative vision. For instance, unlike much conservatism, it rejects constitutional and institutional rigidity, and prescriptive rights. Such established forms should be made functionally efficient. Deliberative procedures should focus on decision-making, and should not waste too much time. The dynamic sources (which were parties and pressure groups in the collectivist age) are think-tanks, planning councils and staffs, and other small expert bodies. Managerial nationalism is not partisan in the conventional sense. It has been carried forward by, and has helped to shape, some aspects of Thatcherism. Looking back, however, it is hard to deny that Sidney and Beatrice Webb were its premature heralds, and obviously some ambitious versions of state socialism fit its values. What could be more managerial than a *National Plan*?[24]

Those who saw the post-war system as the arrival of collectivism can accept and indeed welcome many of the norms of managerial nationalism: it is national in scope and can be seen as a form of adapting to collectivist needs, by making the new institutions efficient. The contrasting market liberators, however, can share the appeal to efficiency, for only free markets can, in their view, ensure allocative efficiency and stimulate technical efficiency. The class struggle goes on, of course: managerial concepts do not change the power of the ruling sector—indeed they make it rather more obvious. And from radical modernisers, the managerial nationalists derive emphasis on executive reform and impatience for change.

It is the conservative sceptics who present most problems. They are not averse to nationalism, interpreted as a continuing tradition. And the instinct for proper authority, the right to manage, is surely the up-to-date version of the old tory philosophy. It is unlike the Old Tory type of politics as explained by S.H. Beer and others,[25] in that it has no connection with a God-given natural order. It is promoted on grounds of functional effectiveness instead—proper authority makes for success. But these conservatives have always thought that rulers should not be afraid to rule. The difficulty lies in the scepticism. The effect of thoroughgoing managerial nationalism would be to turn the state, conceptually, into an enterprise, a body with direction and purpose. In practice the purposes would be largely economic, culminating in a macro-business enterprise.[26] It is hard to see how an Oakeshottian sceptic could view such a conceptualisation as other than a perverse misreading of the true nature of political society.[27]

The prospects of any emerging outlook must be highly speculative. No doubt the various themes will come to terms with the new interpretation some way or other. 'Two languages', then, with managerial nationalism used alongside (at least) four of the five interpretations already diagnosed, is the suggestion offered as a description of the position in the 1980s.

Nevertheless, there is a significant shift of vision—of the image of the object under consideration. Where Bagehot and Dicey saw 'a constitution', the post-war generation saw a 'political system'. What is coming into view, through these new spectacles, is a large functional organisation.

PAST AND PRESENT

The emerging scene is vastly more complex than anything in the foregoing pages can indicate. However, it has been the business of this book to discuss gross simplifications: such rash generalisations have been the material from which the great interpretations were fashioned.

Back at the beginning of the book, review of the works of Mill, Bagehot and Dicey found a sort of running crisis. Most authors had doubts about how the transition to democracy could be managed. By the 1900s crucial steps had been taken, and for many years there was a noticeable sense of relief in the literature. Democracy could be accepted; there was no collapse or real break in continuity; a measure of deference survived; and the problems of politics became those of war and economic change, not of the constitution.

There was then a period in mid-century when socialism appeared as the new challenge, and/or bogey. Would that break the system, as Laski feared, or would it also be accepted without political collapse? For a time, in the post-1945 era, it seemed that ways had been found of adapting to that great transition too.

At present (1988) that particular story is in suspense. Moreover, the status of democracy is not what it was. True, it is universally accepted, to the extent that it now precedes other claims as the first boast of British politicians. Reality and research, however, have confused the dream. Where there was the language of ideals there are now attempts to discover what voting is about—and the answers are abstruse, complex and hard to find—and a set of theories about the nature of democracy, not at all compatible if put into practice.

In Britain (and perhaps elsewhere) it seems that democracy has entered a Machiavellian mode. Fortunately the conventions about violence are not those of Renaissance Italy, but the qualities in demand are not dissimilar. For instance: 'Injuries should be done all together, so that being less tasted, they will give less offence. Benefits should be granted little by little, so that they may be better enjoyed.'[28] The play for power has become a matter of sophisticated skills, of careful timing, of ruthless tactical maneouvres. Elections are openly discussed and reported in these terms: but policy selection by parties and governments is also subjected to such a calculus. Such operations arouse plenty of public interest, as the great game unfolds, but the excitement is that of spectators and rival fans—there is little sense of self-rule.

Insofar as this mode of politics dominates partisan thinking (and it stretches well beyond) it precludes attention to the state of the political system itself. Change in that system is subject to some sort of statecraft—will it enable our party, or indeed our faction of the party to gain power? Politics was ever thus; but the new publicity and the new research of the electronic age have given a new significance to political techniques.

The three questions may be posed for the last time, in relation to managerial nationalism. Does this outlook envisage a sharp break in continuity? It certainly aspires to a change in the rate of economic decline, and a sharp revision of governing structures, in order to strengthen executive power. But the turnaround is to be brought about from the top down: the change avoids political turmoil. What constitutes progress in this vision? There is a ready answer to this question—material betterment, measured in national categories and thereby prestigious. Such an answer, however, reveals more about the interpretation. Both traditionalists and social reformers see political wellbeing in terms of a set of relations to be lived in—for conservatives a regular stable *order,* for socialists a just *society.* For managerialists such things are merely instrumental, and of secondary priority. They should be altered (as often as required) to suit the needs of comparative national efficiency. And so the third answer is self evident: the difference between high politics and low is that the higher level manages the passions of the lower; and activity at the higher level is rationalistic in form.

Managerial nationalism is in the ascendancy, but it is not yet completely dominant. The other outlooks survive. But what is there to stop this outlook, so that eventually it takes over—so that most people imagine the political arrangements of Britain to be those of a purposive organisation for promoting national efficiency?

It may well be that the ascendancy will be checked by its own partial success. The drive to be more efficient will seem less urgent if the international comparisons get better. One way to that would be slowing down in other countries. It is sometimes suggested that alternative calculations might do the trick—British levels of prosperity look better if measured in terms of internal purchasing power.[29] Statistical errors have had their share of influence on history, but it is surely too much to expect that thirty years of trauma can be removed by revising the figures. It is not even clear that new priorities, which gave greater emphasis to environmental factors and work-satisfactions would make all that difference, if they were measured and international comparisons were made. There would be other league tables.

More persuasive is the argument that managerial nationalism leaves out too much. Is it destined to remain a narrow outlook because it cannot cope with the variety of political values and pressures? For instance, in recent decades the number and size of ethnic communities in Britain has brought a major social change: and it must eventually have an impact on the political system. The problem lies with nationalism: can this set of problems be dealt with if the judgements are in terms of efficiency, rather than justice or accommodation? Similar difficulties may arise from the feminist movement. No doubt more women can rise in the hierarchies of organised society; but it seems unlikely that managerial analyses can explain why they have not already done so.

Managerialism tends to be impatient of constitutional forms, seeing them as handicaps to modernisation. At present there is a movement for constitutional reform in Britain, with a programme of electoral reform; freedom of information; a bill of rights; and local government autonomy. It is significant that this programme is promoted on grounds of political efficiency.[30] It, too, claims to reverse or at least restrain the decline of Britain.

In the 1980s while the Government was concerned with making the economy more like that of the United States, reformers were trying to make the polity more like those of European countries. The programme seems a long way from enactment, but (whatever its effects on decline) such a set of changes are at a distance from mere organisational rationalisation. So perhaps different values are around somewhere.

One of the ambitions of Thatcherism in the 1980s was to change the common values of the British, which were allegedly too dependent and unambitious, in the direction of an 'enterprise culture'. This surely has much in common with the ideas of managerial nationalism—at any rate, if such a *Kulturkampf* were successful, then people would increasingly see politics in managerialist terms. Perhaps indeed political conflict in Britain will be increasingly conducted in terms of a clash of cultures, rather than a struggle ultimately concerned with social structure. However, there must be limits to the degree of transformation which managerial efficiency can require of a nation. For has not the idea of a nation become primarily a cultural concept, a way of life? And if too much is changed, then what sort of identity is left, and why should its success matter? Perhaps in the end, managerial nationalism will be self-contradictory. It is not yet in sight of the end. There is a long way to go.

This chapter has already strayed well beyond the bounds of political studies into mere speculation. It is obviously time to bring it to a close.

The examination of interpretations of British arrangements is only a tiny fragment of political affairs. Insofar as the ideas discussed have any wider implications, it is as introductions to the study of political theory proper. Such connections are noted in the *Further Reading*. They will take the reader not only into wider and deeper theoretical matters, but also into other countries, other polities, other traditions. All interpretations need to understand the unique nature of the British system, but they all need to understand its responsiveness and awareness of the external world.

Notes and References

1 INTRODUCTION: THE IMAGE AND THE SYSTEM

1. A.D. Lindsay, *The Modern Democratic State* (Oxford University Press, 1943) Chapter 1.
2. See L. Tivey and A.W. Wright (eds) *Party Ideologies in Britain* (Routledge, 1988).

2 THE FORERUNNERS

1. For general accounts of these periods, see S.H. Beer *Modern British Politics* (Faber 1964) Chapters 1 and 2; and A.H. Birch, *Representative and Responsible Government* (Allen and Unwin 1964) Chapters 2, 3, 4 and 5.
2. See G.H.L. Le May, *The Victorian Constitution* (Duckworth 1979) for a detailed discussion of developments.
3. John Stuart Mill, *Considerations on Representative Government* (1861). References are to the collected edition of the works of J.S. Mill, edited by J.M. Robson and published by the University of Toronto Press and Routledge (1977).
4. J.S. Mill 'Thoughts on Parliamentary Reform' in *Essays on Politics and Society* collected edition vol **, p. 311ff.
5. *ibid* p. 344.
6. *ibid* p. 412.
7. *ibid* p. 467.
8. *ibid* p. 519.
9. Recent editions include Norman St. John Stevas's *Walter Bagehot* (Eyre and Spottiswoode, 1959) which contains 'The English Constitution' in full, with other writings of Bagehot: and the edition published by Fontana in 1963, with an introduction by R.H.S. Crossman. Many of the interpretations by Crossman are perverse. In particular, though Bagehot was clearly intending to denigrate Mill, the 'paper description' attacked by him is not that of Mill (as Crossman alleges), for Mill

145

devalued the 'mixed constitution'—see Chapter 5 in *Representative Government*. Bagehot's real objection to Mill was much simpler—Mill, with precautions, favoured democracy, whereas Bagehot was afraid of it. Page references are to St. John Stevas's edition.

10. *ibid* p. 228.
11. *ibid* p. 228.
12. *ibid* p. 229.
13. *ibid* p. 230.
14. *ibid* p. 231.
15. *ibid* p. 234.
16. *ibid* p. 272.
17. *ibid* p. 306.
18. *ibid* p. 312.
19. *ibid* p. 312.
20. *ibid* p. 312.
21. *ibid* p. 315.
22. *ibid* pp. 331-2.
23. *ibid* p. 363.
24. *ibid* p. 389.
25. *ibid* p. 204.
26. Walter Bagehot, *Physics and Politics* (Kegan Paul, 1872).
27. *ibid* Chapter 3 'Nation-making'.
28. W.E. Hearn, *The Government of England: its Structure and Development* (Longmans Green, London; George Robertson, Melbourne, 1867. Second edition 1886).
29. *ibid* p. 4.
30. *ibid* pp 257-8 and pp 548-50.
31. Thomas Carlyle, 'Shooting Niagara: and after?' (*Macmillan's Magazine,* August 1867).
32. Matthew Arnold, *Culture and Anarchy* (1869.) Edition with introduction by J. Dover Wilson, Cambridge University Press, 1932.
33. Matthew Arnold, 'Stanzas from the Grande Chartreuse' *Arnold: Poetical Works* edited C.B. Tinker and H.F. Lowry (Oxford University Press 1950) p. 302, lines 85-6. Poem first published 1855.
34. Park Honan, *Matthew Arnold: a life* (Weidenfeld 1981) pp 345-9.
35. *Culture and Anarchy,* Chapter 3 'Barbarians, Philistines, Populace'.
36. *ibid* Introduction, p. 41.
37. *ibid* Chapter 2 'Doing as one likes'.
38. James Fitzjames Stephen *Liberty Equality and Fraternity* (Smith, Elder 1874. Reprinted, edited by R.J. White, Cambridge University Press, 1967).
39. W.H. Lecky *Democracy and Liberty* (Longmans Green, 1899).
40. Sir Henry Maine, FRS, *Popular Government* (John Murray, 1885).
41. *ibid* p. 20.
42. *ibid* pp. 35-8.
43. *ibid* p. 51.
44. *ibid* p. 59.
45. *ibid* p. 106.

46. A.V. Dicey, *Lectures introductory to the Study of the Law of the Constitution* (Macmillan, first edition 1885).
47. A.V. Dicey, *Introduction to the Study of the Law of the Constitution* (Macmillan, tenth edition 1959) with introduction by E.C.S. Wade. Page references are to this edition since it is readily available.
48. *ibid* p. 35.
49. *ibid* pp. 202-3.
50. *ibid* p. 23.
51. *ibid* p. 439ff.
52. *ibid* p. 19.
53. *ibid* p. 20.
54. *ibid* p. 73.
55. *ibid* p. 73.
56. A.V. Dicey, *Lectures on the relation between Law and Public Opinion during the nineteenth century* (Macmillan, 1905).
57. *ibid* pp. 12-16.
58. *ibid* Lecture 4, pp. 62-9.
59. *ibid* Lecture 12, pp. 397-463.
60. W. Ivor Jennings, *The Law and the Constitution* (University of London 1933).
    ibid p. 123ff.
62. *ibid* p. 207ff.
63. Richard A. Cosgrove, *The Rule of Law—A. V. Dicey* (Macmillan 1980) Chapter 8, *passim*.
64. Sir William R. Anson, Bart., *The Law and Custom of the Constitution,* three volumes. (Clarendon Press, Oxford, 1886).
65. *ibid* Vol. 1. p. vii.
66. *ibid* p. 13.
67. See Robert Blake, *Disraeli* (Methuen, 1966) pp. 523-4.
68. Sir John R. Seeley, *The Expansion of England* (Macmillan, 1883).
69. *ibid* p. 7.
70. *ibid* p. 9.

3 FURTHER ANTICIPATIONS

1. A.V. Dicey, *Law and Opinion,* p. 48.
2. Sidney Low, *The Governance of England,* (T. Fisher Unwin, 1904).
3. *ibid* p. 3.
4. *ibid* pp. 34-43.
5. *ibid* p. 69.
6. *ibid* p. 93.
7. *ibid* p. 116.
8. *ibid* pp. 174-5.
9. *ibid* p. 175.
10. *ibid* p. 200.
11. *ibid* p. 310.
12. *ibid* pp. 311-2.

13. See B. Semmel, *Imperialism and Social Reform 1895-1914* (Allen and Unwin 1960).
14. Sidney Webb, 'Historic Basis of Socialism' in G. Bernard Shaw (ed.) *Fabian Essays* (Fabian Society, 1889) p. 35.
15. *ibid* p. 35.
16. *ibid* p. 61.
17. C. Tsuzuki, *H.M. Hyndman and British Socialism* (Oxford University Press, 1961).
18. See A. Wright, *Socialisms* (Oxford University Press, 1986).
19. Hilaire Belloc, *The Servile State* (T.N. Foulis, 1912).
20. Moisei Ostrogorski, *Democracy and the Organisation of Political Parties,* two volumes, (Macmillan, 1902).
21. *ibid* p. 120.
22. *ibid* p. 580.
23. *ibid* p. 581.
24. A. Lawrence Lowell, *The Government of England,* two volumes, (Macmillan, 1908).
25. *ibid* vol. 1, pp. 317 and 323.
26. *ibid* p. 431.
27. *ibid* p. 570.
28. *ibid* vol. 2, p. 507.
29. *ibid* p. 508.
30. *ibid* p. 510.
31. *ibid* p. 511.
32. *ibid* pp. 520-30.
33. *ibid* p. 533.
34. *ibid* p. 540.
35. Graham Wallas, *Human Nature in Politics,* (Constable 1908, republished 1948).
36. *ibid* 1948 edition, p. 104.
37. *ibid* p. 118.
38. *ibid* p. 50.
39. *ibid* p. 282ff.
40. *ibid* p. 296.
41. See G.R. Searle, *The Quest for National Efficiency* (Blackwell, 1971).
42. See H. Pelling, *The British Communist Party: a Historical Profile* (Black, 1958), and L.J. Macfarlane, *The British Communist Party: Its Origin and Development until 1929* (Macgibbon and Kee, 1966).
43. Ramsay Muir, *How Britain is Governed* (Constable 1930).
44. Stuart Hodgson (ed.) *Ramsay Muir: an Autobiography and some Essays* (Lund Humphries, 1943).
45. Muir, *How Britain is Governed,* p. 4.
46. *ibid* p. 4.
47. *ibid* p. 35.
48. *ibid* p. 37.
49. *ibid* p. 154.
50. *ibid* pp. 231-2.
51. *ibid* p. 235.

52. *ibid* pp. 108-15.
53. Report on *The Machinery of Government* (Haldane) Cd. 9230, 1918.
54. Muir, *How Britain is Governed* pp. 145-52.
55. *ibid* pp. 177-88.
56. *ibid* pp. 272-3.
57. *ibid* p. 286-9.
58. *ibid* pp. 304-9.
59. *ibid* p. 308.
60. W. Ivor Jennings, *Law and the Constitution* p. 148.
61. *ibid* pp. 137-8.
62. W. Ivor Jennings, *Cabinet Government* (Cambridge University Press, 1936).
63. W. Ivor Jennings, *Parliament* (Cambridge University Press, 1939).
64. Jennings, *Cabinet Government,* p. 1.
65. *ibid* p. 150.
66. *ibid* p. 153.
67. *ibid* p. ix.
68. *ibid* pp. 12-13.
69. *ibid* p. 13.
70. *ibid* p. 15.
71. *ibid* pp. 18-19.
72. Jennings, *Parliament* p. 520.
73. W. Ivor Jennings, *The British Constitution* (Cambridge University Press, fourth edition, 1961).
74. See K. Martin, *Harold Laski 1893-1950* (Gollancz, 1953), and G.G. Eastwood, *Harold Laski* (Mowbrays, 1977).
75. H.J. Laski, *A Grammar of Politics* (Allen and Unwin, 1925); and see D. Nicholls, *The Pluralist State* (Macmillan, 1975).
76. H.J. Laski, *The Crisis and the Constitution* (pamphlet, Hogarth Press and Fabian Society 1932).
77. *ibid* p. 56.
78. H.J. Laski, *Democracy in Crisis* (Allen and Unwin, 1933).
79. *ibid* p. 15.
80. *ibid* p. 83.
81. *ibid* p. 87.
82. H.J. Laski, *Parliamentary Government in England: a Commentary* (Allen and Unwin, 1938).
83. *ibid* p. 84.
84. R. Bassett, *The Essentials of Parliamentary Democracy* (Macmillan, 1935).
85. *ibid* p. 127.
86. W. Ivor Jennings, *The British Constitution* (Cambridge University Press, first edition, June 1941) p. xi.

4 A THEME, WITH VARIATIONS

1. Histories of post-war politics in Britain include P. Calvocoressi, *The*

British Experience 1945-75 (The Bodley Head, 1978), D. Child, *Britain since 1945* (Benn 1979, Methuen 1986), A. Sked and C. Cook *Post-war Britain—a Political History* (Penguin 1979).

2. S.H. Beer, *Modern British Politics* (Faber, 1965 and 1982).
3. *ibid* Introduction, p. xi.
4. *ibid* p. 70.
5. A similar view was propounded by J.A. Schumpeter in *Capitalism, Socialism and Democracy* (Allen and Unwin, 1943) Chapter 22.
6. Contrary to the view of Ramsay Muir, quoted in Chapter 3.
7. Beer, *Modern British Politics* p. 390.
8. S.H. Beer 'Representation of Interests in British Government—Historical Background' *American Political Science Review,* vol. 51, no. 3, September 1957.
9. Beer, *Modern British Politics* p. 387.
10. R.T. McKenzie, *British Political Parties* (Heinemann 1955).
11. R. Michels, *Political Parties* (1915; Dover Publications New York 1959).
12. McKenzie, *British Political Parties* p. 581.
13. *Parliamentary Affairs* vol. 19 no. 3, summer 1966, p. 384.
14. R.T. McKenzie 'Parties, Pressure Groups and the British Political Process' *Political Quarterly,* vol. 29 no. 1, January 1958; frequently reprinted.
15. *ibid* pp. 9-10.
16. H. Eckstein, *Pressure Group Politics* (Allen and Unwin 1960).
17. Allen M. Potter, *Organized Groups in British National Politics* (Faber 1961).
18. S.E. Finer, *Anonymous Empire* (Pall Mall Press, 1958).
19. W. Kornhauser, *The Politics of Mass Society* (Routledge, 1960).
20. A.H. Birch, *Representative and Responsible Government* (Allen and Unwin 1964).
21. *ibid* p. 65. Cf. Dicey's statement in *Law of the Constitution* p. 73.
22. *ibid* p. 165.
23. A.H. Birch *The British System of Government* (Allen and Unwin 1967).
24. Birch, *Representative and Responsible Government* Chapter 13.
25. L.S. Amery, *Thoughts on the Constitution* (Oxford University Press 1947, 1953).
26. *ibid* p. 38.
27. H.J. Laski, *Reflections on the Constitution* (Manchester University Press 1951).
28. For example, K.C. Wheare, *Government by Committee* (Clarendon Press, Oxford, 1955): Wilfrid Harrison, *The Government of Britain* (Hutchinson 1958); Political and Economic Planning, *Advisory Committees in British Government* (Allen and Unwin 1960); W.A. Robson, *Nationalised Industry and Public Ownership* (Allen and Unwin, 1960); D.N. Chester and F.M.G. Willson, *The Organisation of British Central Government 1914-1956* (1957 and 1968).
29. W.J.M. Mackenzie and J.W. Grove, *Central Administration in Britain* (Longman 1957).

30. The pioneering work was R.B. McCallum and A.V. Readman, *The British General Election of 1945* (Macmillan, 1947). In all succeeding volumes David Butler has played a leading part.
31. M. Benney, A.P. Gray and R.H. Pear, *How People Vote* (Routledge 1956).
32. *ibid* p. 6.
33. D.E. Butler and D. Stokes, *Political Change in Britain* (Macmillan 1969, 1974).
34. Ivor Crewe and Bo Sarlvik, *Decade of Dealignment* (Cambridge University Press, 1983).
35. P.J.G. Pulzer, *Political Representation and Elections in Britain* (Allen and Unwin 1967, many editions) p. 98.
36. S.E. Finer, *The Changing British Party System 1945-79* (American Enterprise Institute 1980), D. Robertson, *Class and the British Electorate* (Blackwell 1984) and M. Franklin, *The Decline of Class Voting 1964-79* (Oxford University Press 1985).
37. Notably in terms of 'consumer cleavage' by Patrick Dunleavy and C.T. Husbands *British Democracy at the Crossroads* (Allen and Unwin 1985) and with a new set of classes by A. Heath, R. Jowell and M. Curtice, *How Britain Votes* (Pergamon 1985).
38. J.P. Mackintosh *The British Cabinet* (Stevens, first edition 1962) pp 486-7.
39. J. Blondel, *Voters, Parties and Leaders* (Penguin 1963).
40. R. Rose, *Politics in England* (Faber, first edition 1965).
41. G. Almond, The Politics of the Developing Areas (Viking Press, New York, 1960) pp. 3-64.
42. Rose, *Politics in England* p. 19.
43. *ibid* p. 19.
44. Almond's functional categories were: Input functions—political socialization and recruitment; interest articulation; interest aggregation; political communication. Output functions—rule making; rule application; rule adjudication. *Politics of the Developing Areas* p. 17.
45. S.A. Walkland (ed.) *The House of Commons in the Twentieth Century* (Clarendon Press, Oxford. 1979).
46. A.H. Hanson, 'The Purpose of Parliament' *Parliamentary Affairs* vol. 17 no. 3. Summer 1964.
47. B. Crick *The Reform of Parliament* (Weidenfeld 1964).
48. *ibid* pp. 1-2.
49. *ibid* p. 3.
50. *ibid* p. 259.
51. See G. Drewry (ed.) *The New Select Committees* (Clarendon Press, Oxford 1985).
52. Crick, *Reform of Parliament* p. 46-7.
53. S. Walkland, 'The Politics of Parliamentary Reform' *Parliamentary Affairs* Vol. 29 no. 2 Spring 1976.
54. P. Norton, *Dissension in the House of Common 1974-1979* (Oxford University Press, 1980).

55. A.H. Birch, *The British System of Government* (Allen and Unwin 1967) p. 203.
56. J.P. Mackintosh, *The British Cabinet* (Stevens, first edition 1962).
57. *ibid* p. 451.
58. *ibid* p. 451.
59. Mackintosh, *British Cabinet* second edition 1968, p. 627.
60. R.H.S. Crossman, introduction to W. Bagehot *The English Constitution* p. 54.
61. J. Blondel, *Voters, Parties and Leaders* p. 21.
62. Royal Commission on the Constitution (Kilbrandon) *Report Volume I* (Cmnd. 5460).
63. For example, A.H. Birch, *Political Integration and Disintegration in the British Isles* (Allen and Unwin 1977); M. Kolinsky (ed.) *Divided Loyalties: British Regional Assertion and European Integration* (Manchester University Press 1978); V. Bogdanor *Devolution* (Oxford University Press, 1979); R. Rose, *Northern Ireland—a Time of Choice* (Macmillan 1976) and *Understanding the United Kingdom* (Longman 1982).
64. C. Cook and D. McKie (ed.) *The Decade of Disillusion* (Macmillan 1972).
65. L. Tivey 'The Political Consequences of Economic Planning' *Parliamentary Affairs* vol. 20. no. 4 Autumn 1967.
66. See Wyn Grant 'Corporatism and Pressure Groups' in D. Kavanagh and R. Rose (eds) *New Trends in British Politics* (Sage 1977) pp. 167-90 for a critical account.
67. K. Middlemas, *Politics in Industrial Society* (Andre Deutsch 1979).
68. *ibid* Chapter 13.
69. R.E. Pahl and J. Winkler 'The Coming Corporatism' *New Society* 10 October 1974.
70. Wyn Grant (ed.) *Political Economy of Corporatism* (Macmillan, 1985).
71. J.J. Richardson and A.G. Jordan, *Governing under Pressure* (Martin Robertson 1979).
72. *ibid* Preface p. vii.
73. *ibid* p. 191.
74. *ibid* p. 192.
75. B. Hogwood *From Crisis to Complacency?* (Oxford University Press 1987).
76. Reprinted in the Fulton Report—*Report on the Civil Service Vol. 1* (Cmnd. 3638) Appendix B. p. 108.
77. Richard Rose 'Still the Era of Party Government' *Parliamentary Affairs* vol. 36 no. 3. Summer 1983 p. 282.
78. Alan Beattie 'The two-party Legend' *Political Quarterly* vol. 45 no. 3. July 1974.
79. S.E. Finer (ed.) *Adversary Politics and Electoral Reform* (Wigram 1975).
80. O. Hood Phillips, *Reform of the Constitution* (Chatto and Windus 1970. Chapter 7. N. Johnson, *In Search of the Constitution* (Pergamon 1977); Lord Hailsham, *The Dilemma of Democracy* (Collins 1978).

81. See Richard Chapman and Michael Hunt (eds) *Open Government* (Croom Helm 1987) for a general account.
82. P. Holland and M. Fallon, *The Quango Explosion* (Conservative Political Centre, 1978); and Anthony Barker (ed.) *Quangos in Britain* (Macmillan 1982).
83. S.H. Beer, *Britain Against Itself* (Faber 1982).
84. A. King, 'Overload: Problems of Governing in the 1970s' *Political Studies* vol. 23 nos 2-3 (1975).
85. A. King (ed.) *Why is Britain Harder to Govern?* (B.B.C. publications, 1976) p. 14.
86. *ibid* p. 14.
87. *ibid* p. 15.
88. *ibid* p. 29.

5 OTHER THEMES, AND DISCORDS

1. Michael Oakeshott 'Political Education' in *Rationalism in Politics* (Methuen 1962) p. 127. In the original print of the lecture, published by Bowes and Bowes, Cambridge 1951, p. 22, the final phrase was '. . . every inimical occasion.'
2. N. Johnson, *In Search of the Constitution* (Pergamon 1977) pp. 3-4.
3. *ibid* p. 5.
4. *ibid* Chapters 11 and 12.
5. E. Kedourie, 'A New International Disorder' in *Crossman's Confessions and other essays* (Mansell 1984) pp. 102-103.
6. N. Johnson, *In Search of the Constitution* p. 38.
7. C.H. Sisson *The Spirit of British Administration* (Faber 1959) p. 23.
8. See J.P. Bulpitt, 'Mrs. Thatcher's Domestic Statecraft' in *Political Studies* No. 34, no. 1. March 1986.
9. D. Hurd, *An end to promises* (Collins 1979).
10. S. Letwin, 'On Conservative Individualism' in M. Cowling (ed.) *Conservative Essays* (Cassell, 1978) p. 61.
11. W.H. Greenleaf 'The Character of Modern British Politics' *Parliamentary Affairs* vol. 28 no. 4, Autumn 1975, p. 374.
12. *ibid* p. 375.
13. A.V. Dicey, *Lectures on the Relation between Law and Public Opinion in England during the Nineteenth century* (Macmillan, 1905).
14. W.H. Greenleaf, *The British Political Tradition Volume 2 The Ideological Heritage* (Methuen 1983).
15. *ibid* pp. 14-15.
16. *ibid* p. 15.
17. F.A. Hayek, *The Road to Serfdom* (Routledge 1944, 1976).
18. *ibid* p. 10.
19. *ibid* p. 15.
20. *ibid* pp. 2-7 and pp. 135-7.
21. F.A. Hayek, *The Constitution of Liberty* (Routledge 1960).
22. *ibid* p. 398. Contrast the attitude of Oakeshott noted in the previous section.

23. For example: Milton Friedman and Anna Schwarz, *A Monetary History of the United State 1867-1960* (Princeton University Press 1963) and M. Friedman, *The Counter Revolution in Monetary Theory* (Institute of Economic Affairs 1970).
24. S. Brittan, *Capitalism and the Permissive Society* (Macmillan 1973).
25. S. Brittan, *Role and Limits of Government* (Temple Smith 1977) p. 50.
26. S. Brittan, *The Economic Consequence of Democracy* (Temple Smith 1977).
27. *ibid* p. 247.
28. *ibid* p. 266.
29. *ibid* pp. 267-77.
30. *ibid* p. 257.
31. *ibid* p. 253.
32. H.S. Ferns, *The Disease of Government* (Temple Smith 1978).
33. *ibid* p. 122.
34. Lord Hailsham, *The Dilemma of Democracy* (Collins 1978) p. 132.
35. *ibid* p. 226.
36. *ibid* p. 222.
37. J. O'Connor, *The Fiscal Crisis of the State* (St. James' Press, New York 1973).
38. R. Miliband, *Parliamentary Socialism* (Allen and Unwin 1961, Merlin 1973).
39. R. Miliband, *The State in Capitalist Society* (Weidenfeld, 1969).
40. *ibid* p. 78.
41. R. Miliband, *Capitalist Democracy in Britain* (Oxford University Press, 1982).
42. *ibid* Preface p.v.
43. *ibid* p. 1.
44. *ibid* pp. 148-60.
45. D. Coates *Labour in Power?* (Longman, 1980).
46. *ibid* p. 265.
47. *ibid* p. 279.
48. T. Nairn 'The nature of the British State' in D. Coates and J. Hillard (eds) *The Economic Decline of Modern Britain* (Wheatsheaf Books 1986) p. 239.
49. J. Harvey and K. Hood (pseud.) *The British State* (Lawrence and Wishart, 1958) p. 9.
50. John Callaghan, *British Trotskyism* (Blackwell 1984).
51. A. Gamble, *The Conservative Nation* (Routledge, 1974).
52. *ibid* p. 218.
53. A. Gamble, *Britain in Decline* (Macmillan 1981, 1985).
54. *ibid* p. 84.
55. *ibid* p. 98.
56. *ibid* p. 98.
57. A. Kilpatrick and T. Lawson 'The Strength of the Working Class' in D. Coates and J. Hillard (eds) *The Economic Decline of Modern Britain* pp. 250-8.
58. J. Dearlove and P. Saunders, *Introduction to British Politics* (Polity Press, 1984).

59. *ibid* p. 5.
60. *ibid* p. 116.
61. *ibid* p. 218.
62. Report of the Committee in *The Civil Service Volume 1* (Fulton) (Cmnd. 3638).
63. *ibid* p. 9.
64. M. Shanks, *The Stagnant Society* (Penguin 1961).
65. *ibid* pp. 13-14.
66. *ibid* p. 29.
67. B. Chapman, *British Government Observed* (Allen and Unwin 1963).
68. *ibid* p. 27.
69. *ibid* p. 60.
70. A Shonfield, *Modern Capitalism* (Oxford University Press 1965).
71. *ibid* p. 386.
72. J. Hayward, 'Institutional Inertia and Political Impetus in France and Britain' *European Journal of Political Research* vol. 4 no. 4. December 1976, p. 351.
73. B. Chapman, *British Government Observed,* p. 12.
74. A. Shonfield, *Modern Capitalism* p. 387.
75. P. Kellner and Lord Crowther-Hunt, *The Civil Servants* (Macdonald Futura 1980).
76. *ibid* p. 9.
77. B. Chapman, *The Profession of Government* (Allen and Unwin 1959).
78. B. Chapman, *British Government Observed* p. 19.
79. M. Shanks, *The Stagnant Society* p. 100.
80. M. Young, *The Rise of the Meritocracy 1870-2033* (Thames and Hudson 1958).
81. Daniel Bell, *The End of Ideology* (Collier Macmillan 1960) and *The Coming of Post-Industrial Society* (Heinemann 1974).
82. C. Barnett *The Collapse of British Power* (Morrow, New York, 1972).
83. C. Barnett, *The Audit of War* (Macmillan 1986).
84. *ibid* Preface p. xi.
85. M. Wiener, *English Culture and the Decline of the Industrial Spirit 1850-1980* (Cambridge University Press 1981).
86. *ibid* Chapter 6.
87. B. Chapman *British Government Observed p. 10.*

6 AN EMERGING INTERPRETATION

1. A.L. Lowell, *The Government of England,* two volumes (Macmillan 1908).
2. H.J. Laski, *Parliamentary Government in England* (Allen and Unwin 1938).
3. The widening of the *institutional* range of recent political studies, as begun by Dearlove and Saunders, or Richardson and Jordan, is relevant.
4. A.V. Dicey, *Law of the Constitution,* p. 73.
5. W.H. Greenleaf, *Ideological Heritage* and elsewhere. See also A.O.

Hirschman, *Shifting Involvements* (Martin Robertson 1982) for an economist's explanation of these fluctuations.

6. House of Lords *Hansard,* 30 June 1987, col. 185.
7. M. Bentley and J. Stevenson (eds) *High and Low Politics in Modern Britain* (Clarendon Press, Oxford 1983).
8. *ibid* p. 59.
9. A.M. Gamble and S.A. Walkland, *The British Party System and Economic Policy 1945-1983* (Clarendon Press Oxford 1984) Preface, p. ix.
10. E.A. Shils, *The Torment of Secrecy* (Heinemann, 1956).
11. *ibid* p. 55.
12. R. Hofstadter *The Paranoid Style in American Politics* (Cape, 1966).
13. For instance: S. Hall and M. Jacques (eds) *The Politics of Thatcherism* (Lawrence and Wishart 1983); D. Kavanagh, *Thatcherism and British Politics* (Oxford University Press, 1987); and K. Minogue and M. Biddiss (eds) *Thatcherism: Personality and Politics* (Macmillan 1987).
14. A.M. Gamble, *The Free Economy and the Strong State* (Macmillan 1988).
15. E. Shils, *Torment of Secrecy,* p. 56.
16. For instance, L. Epstein 'What happened to the British Party Model?' *American Political Science Review,* vol. 74 no. 1. March 1980.
17. Institute of Economic Affairs, *Rebirth of Britain* (Pan Books, 1964).
18. Committee of Vice-Chancellors and Principals, *Report of the Steering Committee for Efficiency Studies in Universities* (Jarratt), (CVCP, March 1985).
19. G.R. Searle, *The Quest for National Efficiency—a Study in British Politics and Political Thought 1899-1914* (Blackwell, Oxford, 1971).
20. William James, 'The moral flabbiness born of the bitch goddess SUCCESS . . .' Letter to H.G. Wells, 11 September 1906.
21. T. Stephenson, *Management: a Political Activity* (Macmillan, 1985).
22. *ibid* Preface p. vii.
23. *ibid* Introduction p. 1x.
24. Department of Economic Affairs, *The National Plan* (Cmnd. 2764, 1965).
25. S.H. Beer, *Modern British Politics,* Chapter 1.
26. See L. Tivey, 'States, Nations and Economies', in L. Tivey (ed.) *The Nation-State* (Martin Robertson, 1981).
27. See M. Oakeshott, *On Human Conduct* (Oxford University Press, 1975) Part III.
28. N. Machiavelli, *The Prince* (1532 trans. L. Ricci 1903) (Oxford University Press, 1935) Chapter 8.
29. For instance, *National Accounts, 1987 edition, volume 1* Organisation for Economic Co-operation and Development (Paris, 1987).
30. As in Richard Holme, 'Better Government' *Parliamentary Affairs* vol. 40, no. 4, October 1987.

Further Reading

There is a vast literature on British politics, and a large proportion of it impinges in some way or other on the subject of this book. This list is intended to lead the reader to those works particularly relevant to general conceptions of the system, rather than to particular aspects.

THE CLASSICS

Serious students will read the great books for themselves. John Stuart Mill's *Considerations on Representative Government* (1861) is available in many editions: in the *Collected Works* (ed. J.M. Robson) it is in *Essays on Politics and Society* Vol. XIX (University of Toronto Press, 1977). Walter Bagehot's *The English Constitution* (1867) is in volume 5 of the *Collected Works* (ed. N. St. John Stevas; The Economist, London, 1974); in N. St. John Stevas's *Walter Bagehot* (Eyre and Spottiswoode, 1959); and in an edition introduced by R.H.S. Crossman (Fontana 1963, Watts 1964). A.V. Dicey's *Introduction to the Study of the Law of the Constitution* (1885) is published by Macmillan with an introduction by E.C.S. Wade (tenth edition 1959, many reprints). Matthew Arnold's *Culture and Anarchy* (1869) is available in a Cambridge University Press edition of 1932, many reprints. Other essentials are Sir Henry Maine's *Popular Government— four essays* (1885, popular edition John Murray 1909; Liberty Fund, Indianopolis 1976), and Sir J.R. Seeley, *The Expansion of England* (Macmillan, 1883; University of Chicago, 1971).

For background to this scene, read G. le May, *The Victorian Constitution* (Duckworth, 1979); Robert Pearson and Geraint Williams, *Political Thought and Public Policy in the Nineteenth Century* (Longman, 1984); and Martin Pugh, *The Making of Modern British Politics 1867-1939* (Blackwell, 1982). For a vivid introduction, read the dialogue 'Democracy' in M. Cranston, *Political Dialogues* (BBC Publications, 1968).

Later interpretations include Sidney Low, *The Governance of England* (Fisher Unwin 1904, many reprints) and A. Lawrence Lowell, *The Government of England* (two volumes, Macmillan, 1908). Early analysis of democracy in practice is found in Mosei Ostrogorski, *Democracy and the Organisation of Political Parties,* volume 1, (Macmillan, 1902) and in Graham Wallas, *Human Nature in Politics* (Constable, 1908, reprinted 1948).

For the period between the wars the essential reading includes Ramsay Muir, *How Britain is Governed* (Constable, 1930); and from the many works of Harold J. Laski, *Democracy in Crisis* (Allen and Unwin, 1933) and *Parliamentary Government in England* (Allen and Unwin, 1938). The best impressions of Sir Ivor Jennings's version are probably gained from *Law and the Constitution* (University of London Press, 1933) and from *Cabinet Government* (Cambridge University Press, 1936).

THE COLLECTIVIST PERIOD

The post-war classics are led by S.H. Beer, *Modern British Politics* (Faber, 1965 and 1982. In the United States entitled *Politics in the Collectivist Age*); and by A.H. Birch, *Representative and Responsible Government* (Allen and Unwin, 1964). In addition to major contributions in their own right, these two books give valuable accounts, in their early chapters, of political conceptions in Britain before those of liberal democracy.

Other important works of the period deal with particular aspects, and show the variations on the theme. Works of this type include R.T. McKenzie, *British Political Parties* (Heinemann 1955, many reprints); Bernard Crick, *The*

Reform of Parliament (Weidenfeld 1964, 1968); and J.P. Mackintosh, *The British Cabinet* (Stevens, first edition 1962, revised in 1968 and 1977). The voting studies which tried to explain democratic reality can be represented by D. Butler and D. Stokes, *Political Change in Britain* (Macmillan 1969, revised 1974) and by Ivor Crewe and Bo Sarlvik, *The Decade of Dealignment* (Cambridge University Press, 1983). For pressure groups read R.T. McKenzie's early article 'Parties, Pressure Groups and the British Political Process' *Political Quarterly* Vol. 29, no. 1 January 1958, and the much later book by G. Jordan and J. Richardson, *Government and Pressure Groups in Britain* (Clarendon Press, Oxford, 1987). The persistence of meso-corporatism is explained in Wyn Grant (ed.) *The Political Economy of Corporatism* (Macmillan, 1985), especially introduction by Grant. Not to be missed is the study of 'post-Parliamentary democracy' by J.J. Richardson and G. Jordan, *Governing under Pressure* (Martin Robertson, 1979), followed by their *British Politics and the Policy Process* (Allen and Unwin, 1987). An interpretation in itself is in Richard Rose, *Politics in England* (Faber, 1980 edition). Douglas Ashford explored *Policy and Politics in Britain—the Limits of Consensus* (Blackwell, 1981).

For imperialism in retreat, read John Darwin, *Britain and Decolonisation 1945-65* (Macmillan, 1985); and for foreign policy, F. Northedge, *Descent from Power—British Foreign Policy 1945-73* (Allen and Unwin, 1974).

OTHER THEMES

The scene looked different from different points of vantage. Read Michael Oakeshott *Rationalism in Politics* (Methuen 1962) to locate one such viewpoint; and Maurice Cowling (ed.) *Conservative Essays* (Cassell 1978) for more in this direction. An essay which might (or might not) fit in this school is Nevil Johnson's *In Search of the Constitution* (Pergamon, 1977). There is no understanding of market liberation without reading F.A. Hayek, *The Road to Serfdom* (Routledge 1944, reprinted 1976). For the British case read Samuel Brittan *Capitalism and the Permissive Society* (Macmillan, 1973) and

The Economic Consequences of Democracy (Temple Smith, 1977). A Marxist version of the class-conflict view is clearly and forcefully set out in Ralph Miliband's *Capitalist Democracy in Britain* (Oxford University Press, 1982) which followed his broader thesis in *The State in Capitalist Society* (Weidenfeld, 1969). For an illustration of how such an outlook affects interpretation, read David Coates *Labour in Power?* (Longman, 1980). Other interpretations paying attention to class and property relations are Andrew Gamble *Britain in Decline* (Macmillan 1982) and John Dearlove and Peter Saunders's indecisive thesis in *Introduction to British Politics* (Polity Press 1984). P. Dunleavy and C.T. Husbands *British Democracy at the Crossroads* (Allen and Unwin 1985) offered an alternative analysis of social cleavage. The radicals of the 1960s, collectivist inclined, included Michael Shanks, *The Stagnant Society* (Penguin 1961) and Andrew Shonfield *Modern Capitalism* (Oxford University Press, 1965) following an earlier pamphlet, *British Government Observed* (Allen and Unwin 1963) by Brian Chapman. Later, cultural radicalism followed from Martin Wiener's history *English Culture and the Decline of the Industrial Spirit 1850-1980* (Cambridge University Press, 1981, Penguin 1985).

MANAGERIALISM AND NATIONALISM

Managerialism may have deep roots in the works of Plato and Machiavelli, but the search for them is likely to lead to misunderstanding of those philosphers. Similarly some have professed to find origins of managerialism in the work of Saint-Simon; but see Ghita Ionescu, *The Political Thought of Saint-Simon* (Oxford University Press, 1976). One version of the phenomenon was proclaimed by James Burnham in *The Managerial Revolution* (1941, reprinted Greenwood Press, 1972): and another, described as a technostructure, was discerned by J.K. Galbraith in *The New Industrial State* (Hamish Hamilton 1967). But as relevant to the developments noted in this book as anything is W.H. Whyte, *The Organisation Man* (Jonathan Cape 1957). The early rise of efficiency as a political value is described by G.B. Searle in *The*

Quest for National Efficiency 1899-1914 (Blackwell 1971). In Trevor Smith *Anti-Politics* (C. Knight, 1972) a relevant critique is expressed.

Nationalism has a large literature, not enough of it concerned with the British case. A. Cobban described *The Nation State and National Self-determination* (Collins 1969, earlier version Oxford University Press 1945). Elie Kedourie explored its origins in *Nationalism* (Hutchinson, 1960): A.D. Smith elucidated *Theories of Nationalism* (Duckworth, 1971), and Hugh Seton-Watson recounted history in *Nations and States* (Methuen, 1977). These and other writers provide foundation reading. In L. Tivey (ed.) *The Nation-State* (Martin Robertson 1981) contributors explore the ramifications of this phenomenon, including an essay by Tivey on 'States, Nations and Economies'. The state can indeed be analysed as an enterprise: see R.D. Auster and M. Silver, *The State as a Firm—Economic Forces in Political Development* (Martinus Nijhoff, The Hague, 1979).

ARTICLES AND ESSAYS

There is a vast flow of specialised material: noted here are some articles which attempt general assessments.

W.H. Greenleaf's thesis is set out in 'The Character of Modern British Government' *Parliamentary Affairs* vol. 28 no. 4, Autumn 1975; and W.J.M. Mackenzie gave an account of 'Models of English Politics' in R. Rose (ed.) *Studies in British Politics* (Macmillan, third edition 1976).

Andrew Gamble forecast 'The Future of British Politics' in *Parliamentary Affairs,* vol. 35 no. 4, Autumn 1982; and in the same issue John Dearlove reviewed 'The Political Science of British Politics'; and Wayne Parsons wrote on 'Politics without Promises'.

A.W. Wright asked 'What Sort of Crisis?' in the *Political Quarterly,* vol. 8 no. 3, July 1977; and ten years later asked 'British Decline—Political or Economic?' in *Parliamentary Affairs,* vol. 40, no. 1, January 1987. Richard Rose put the question 'Ungovernability: is there Fire behind the Smoke?' in *Political Studies,* vol. 27 no. 3, September 1979. These problems were reviewed by A.H. Birch in 'Overload, Ungovernability and Delegitimation—the Theories and the British Case' in the *British Journal of Political Science,* vol. 14, no. 2, April 1984. Dennis Kavanagh's question was 'Whatever happened to Consensus Politics?' *Political Studies,* vol. 33, no. 4, December 1985. David Held explained the route from 'Stability to Crisis in Post-war Britain' in *Parliamentary Affairs,* vol. 40, no. 2, April 1987.

Trevor Smith discussed 'Political Science and Modern British Society' in *Government and Opposition,* vol. 21, no. 4, Autumn 1986. J.C. Rees' lecture 'Interpreting the Constitution' is in Preston King (ed.) *The Study of Politics* (Cass, 1977). Long ago Leonard Tivey wrote about 'The System of Democracy in Britain' *Sociological Review,* vol. 6, no. 1, July 1958. Thomas J. Carberry noted 'The Americanisation of British Politics' in the *Journal of Politics* (University of Florida) vol. 27, no. 1, February 1965. Dennis Kavanagh wrote on 'An American Science of British Politics' in *Political Studies,* vol. 22 no. 3, September, 1974.

In G. McLennan, D. Held and S. Hall (eds) *State and Society in Contemporary Britain* (Polity Press 1984) the essays by Stuart Hall and by David Held offer general perspectives; and in J. Hayward and P. Norton (eds) *The Political Science of British Politics* (Wheatsheaf Books 1986) there are general observations by Jack Hayward and Trevor Smith. The collection by J. Jowell and D. Oliver (eds) *The Changing Constitution* (Clarendon Press, Oxford, 1985) contains a general essay by A.H. Birch.

WIDER POLITICS

It would be absurd to suggest that interpretations and images bear anything but a loose relation to the political theories that they reflect and distort. Readers, however, can move on.

A first step can be taken with an old book: A.D. Lindsay, *The Modern Democratic State* (Oxford University Press 1946, paperback 1962). More about British ideas can be learned from A.V. Dicey's lectures on *Law and Opinion* (Macmillan 1905), and from a successor volume edited by Morris Ginsberg, *Law and Opinion in England in the Twentieth Century* (Stevens 1959). Again, W.H. Greenleaf's four volumes *The British Political Tradition* (Methuen, from 1983) offer rich fare. Rodney Barker's *Political Ideas in Modern Britain* (Methuen 1978) provides a guide to the twentieth century. L. Tivey and A. Wright (eds) *Party Ideology in Britain* (Routledge, 1988) is a short introduction to recent ideas and policies.

The schools of political theory most sympathetic to the collectivist arrival theme were pluralist and social democratic. G. Almond and S. Verba in *The Civic Culture* (Princeton University Press, 1963) presented an analysis in which the British model fitted well. In *The Civic Culture Revisited* (Little Brown, Boston, 1980) they had more to tell. The most relevant American version of pluralism was developed by Robert A. Dahl: see *Polyarchy—Participation and Opposition* (Yale University Press, 1971). Party democracy followed J.A. Schumpeter's model in *Capitalism, Socialism and Democracy* (Allen and Unwin, 1943) Part 4. The best notion of J.M. Keynes's political approach, as distinct from the implications of his economics, can be found in *Essays in Persuasion* (Macmillan 1931): and in *Collected Works Volume 9,* (Macmillan 1972), particularly 'The End of *Laissez-faire*'. An attempt to save and revise socialist ideas in the middle of the period was made by C.A.R. Crosland in *The Future of Socialism* (Cape, 1956). For the exhaustion of political ideas in the fifties, read Daniel Bell, *The End of Ideology* (Collier Macmillan, 1960). Many hoped to find a renewed rationale for political judgements in John Rawls, *A Theory of Justice* (Oxford University Press, 1972). The theory of corporatism was revived in P.C. Schmitter and G. Lehmbruch (eds) *Trends toward Corporatist Intermediation* (Sage 1979).

Important conservative works include Michael Oakeshott *On Human Conduct* (Oxford University Press, 1975); Roger Scruton, *The Meaning of Conservatism* (Penguin 1980) and K. Minogue, *Alien Powers* (Weidenfeld 1985). F.A. Hayek's later writings are in *Law, Legislation and Liberty* (three volumes, Routledge, from 1973). Dan Usher, *The Economic Prerequisite to Democracy* (Blackwell, 1985) and Mancur Olson, *The Rise and Decline of Nations* (Yale University Press, 1982) contributed to new suspicions of the state. Public choice theory, such as J. Buchanan and G. Tullock, *The Calculus of Consent* (University of Michigan, 1962) and philosophy by Robert Nozick, *Anarchy, State and Utopia* (Blackwell 1974) added to the deconstruction. Marxism was refreshed in post-war years by the publication of *The Prison Notebooks* of A. Gramsci (Lawrence and Wishart 1971) and the fecundity of its variants was assured by (for instance) L. Althusser, *For Marx* (Penguin 1969); J. Habermas, *Legitimation Crisis* (Heinemann 1976); and N. Poulantzas, *State, Power, Socialism* (New Left Books, 1978).

For an introduction to contemporary theory, read Patrick Dunleavy and Brendan O'Leary, *Theories of the State* (Macmillan 1987), a guide with many merits, not least that its classification (pluralism, new right, elite theory, Marxism, neo-pluralism) avoids simplistic dichotomies.

Index